CAGE & AVIARY BIRDS

CAGE & AVIARY
BIRDS

T. VRIENDS

TREASURE PRESS

First published in Great Britain in 1980 by Ward Lock Limited

This edition published in 1990 by
Treasure Press
Michelin House
81 Fulham Road
London
SW3 6RB

Translated by Maria Taylor
Layout by Peter Holroyd

ISBN 1 85051 445 3

Printed in: Edições ASA - Portugal

Acknowledgements

The photographs in the book have been supplied by the following:
Wilko Bergmans, Bernsen's International Press Service Ltd,
Zdenek Burian, Bruce Coleman Ltd, P. Leysen, A. van den
Nieuwenhuizen, Popperfoto, Cees Scholtz, Archiv Smeets, Pim
Smit, Fotoarchiv Spaarnstadt, and P. Zwister

Contents

1 History and evolution

Aviculture is a hobby which gives many people great pleasure. It provides an opportunity not only to observe and study birds at close range, but also to enjoy their lively songs and brilliant colours. If birds are made to feel comfortable and at ease they will show themselves at their finest. For this reason it is important to know about their particular characteristics, habits and general requirements, because their captive conditions must represent, as closely as possible, those to which they are accustomed in the wild.

Before considering the particular care required by the various kinds of birds that are kept in captivity, it is worth having a quick look at the way in which birds may have evolved from a reptilian ancestor nearly 200 million years ago. The word 'evolution' means 'gradual change' and although humans have understood for many centuries that it takes place, it is only recently – during this century – that they have come to understand the genetic mechanisms involved.

The theory of evolution by natural selection was first expounded by Charles Darwin (1809-1882) in 1859 when his famous book, 'The Origin of Species' was published. In it he showed that the gradual change of simple forms of life into

Left The Pekin Robin (*Leiothrix lutea*) is an excellent singer with five to seven verses in its repertoire

Right The male Blue-winged Pitta (*Pitta moluccensis*)

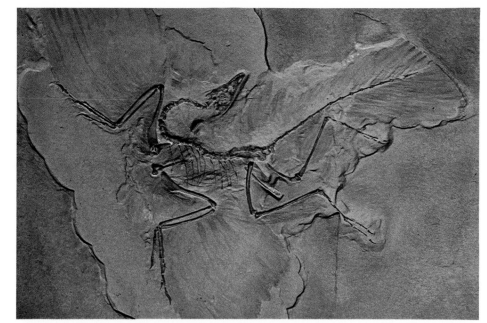

Right Fossil of the earliest known bird *Archaeopteryx*, which must have lived approximately 140 million years ago. This limestone fossil shows that not all prehistoric animals were of gigantic size. This bird ancestor was no bigger than a magpie

Above A splendid reconstruction of the ancestral bird, *Archaeopteryx*

Right Pterodactyls were flying saurians which conquered the air after the insects and before the birds. They were able to flutter like bats by means of membranous webbing between their limbs and body trunks

An ancestor of diving birds, *Hesperornis regalis*, shows a surprising similarity to present-day divers. Like today's penguin it had totally lost the power of flight. The nearly two-metre (6ft) long *Hesperornis* had only small wing-stumps, a pointed beak and knifesharp teeth with which it probably killed cuttle-fish

A bird skeleton – here that of a duck – strongly resembles a mammal's. Where it differs is in its adaptation to flight. This skeleton is noticeable for its firmness and its minimal weight

The female African Paradise Flycatcher (*Terpsiphone viridis*) builds a nest consisting, among other things, of spiderwebs

The nest of the Common Coot (*Fulica atra*). On the offspring one can see clearly the egg teeth with which they break open their egg shells. As soon as the chicks have hatched out, these teeth fall off

more complex ones might have been brought about by a succession of small steps covering millions of years.

This theory, which is now universally accepted, provides an explanation for the adaptation of plants and animals to their environments, and it further implies that if an organism is not well adapted it will soon become extinct. But environments usually change slowly (Continental Drift is a good example of this) and organisms adapt over successive generations of genetic mutation.

As a result of this lengthy process, the last few hundred million years have seen a multitude of plants and animal species gradually evolving.

The process by which species evolve is highly complex and difficult to understand without a thorough appreciation of the genetic mechanisms of inheritance. But a simplified explanation is possible, especially if we consider only those animals which reproduce sexually (as opposed to asexually when only one adult produces offspring). Birds reproduce sexually and for this purpose male and female adults combine their genetic material in the form of a hard-shelled egg which is incubated outside the body (they are therefore said to be oviparous). The developing chick is made up of characteristics of both parents and, although it will grow to be very like them, it will carry what are

Right You will encounter the St Helena Waxbill (*Estrilda astrild*) on St Helena, in Africa and on surrounding islands. This bird which is also called 'Common Waxbill' should be kept in a spacious aviary

Below A Fire Finch (*Lagonosticta senegala*) and a Cordon Bleu (*Uraeginthus bengalus*) drink side by side from a puddle in Kenya

called individual differences. This is because things can go wrong in the process by which one chick is made up from the characteristics of two adults. The 'wrong' bit is called a mutation and yet sometimes it can actually be beneficial to the offspring that carries it. This chick might find that its mutation enabled it to see better than others around it. It would, therefore, be able to spot food or predators first and this factor would increase its survival chances. Increased survivial gives it a better chance of breeding and, because the advantageous mutation has become a fixed part of its genetic make up, its own offspring will inherit genes for better vision. And so it goes on, generation after generation with mutations occurring in all parts of the body until some groups of individuals have changed in a way that not only makes them unrecognisable as closely related to the species to which they once belonged, but also unable to breed with any living individuals from that species. They have, in effect, formed a new species.

Today, some 8600 bird species exist. There were once many more than that, perhaps a third as many again, but they have declined in the last few million years. All the countless subspecies of bird are simply changes being presently undertaken within species groups. In other words, a subspecies is a

The Blue Tanager (*Thraupis episcopus*) occurs in South America to a height of 2500 metres (6,900ft). The sexes look alike

Superb Tanager (*Tangara fastuosa*) from
Brazil. The colours of this bird are
overwhelmingly beautiful, but its song is
less alluring

recognisable trend within a species towards the formation of a new species.
Hybrid zones are made up when changing individuals breed with the
individuals belonging to the original stock.

Another example can be drawn from the reptiles. Lizards once lived
primarily on the ground with lots of other different kinds of animal. Some of the
lizards would have started to venture up the rough bark of trees. Many of them
couldn't have stayed there for long because they were better suited to running
over the earth below. But mutations for long sharp claws would have given
tree-climbing advantages to some of them. In the trees they would have found
insects and safety from ground-dwelling predators; in other words, their
chances of survival and reproduction were increased. Their offspring carried
their same mutation and obviously lived in the tree-climbing way of their
parents. But now that they were in the trees other mutations were occurring and
being selected for. They grew to look very different from their ground-dwelling
ancestors. In time, new species were formed.

It is quite a good idea to have looked at a way of reptile evolution, because it
was from this group of animals that birds evolved some 160 million years ago. It
is a complicated process and one about which we do not know a great deal.

The Louisiana Tanager (*Piranga
ludoviciana*) lives in the western part of
the USA. It spends the winter in Central
America

The Gouldian Finch (red-headed variety)
(*Chloebia gouldiae*) in flight. This bird's
food consists mainly of seeds, termites,
spiders and beetles which it looks for in
the dry Savannah and Eucalyptus woods
in Northern Australia

13

Left and right The Lavender Finch (*Estrilda caerulescens*) during pairing time. The red tail plays an important part during the love dance. This bird occurs in an area which stretches from Senegal to the south of Lake Chad

However, we can get some idea of the events that took place by tracing the outline of development.

220 million years ago the dry land was inhabited by insects, amphibians and reptiles. The latter group included the Thecodonts which were lizard-like creatures with very long tails. One group of Thecodonts adapted to life in the trees, with their forelegs becoming useful for climbing. In general their limbs enabled them to jump from branch to branch until they were quite at home many metres above the ground.

At some stage their reptilian scales began to adopt a feathery appearance. This may have been to increase their insulaton against cooling temperatures, but, whatever the reason, the tree-dwelling reptile became lighter and more able to undertake spectacular leaps from branch to branch and even from tree to tree. As they jumped they beat their feathery forelegs and this increased the distance they could travel through the air. The advantages of being able to do this were evidently selected for (perhaps they could out-distance predators or out-distance competitors for food) and their appearance became genetically 'fixed'. It was from this kind of beginning that birds evolved from reptiles.

The earliest known bird is *Archaeopteryx lithographica*, which means 'ancient

Lybius leucomelas from South Africa feeds on berries and other fruit. The young ones are reared on insects

The Green Humming Bird (*Chlorostilbon mellisugus*) which occurs on Aruba, Curacao and Bonaire, is approximately 8cm (3in) long. The female is not as colourful as the male. Some humming birds can beat their wings 50 times per second whereas the wing beat speed of most birds is only 2-10 per second

The Yellow-fronted Tinker Bird (*Pogoniulus chrysoconus*) from Africa is well known because of its hour-long singing concerts

Above right The Red-throated Twin-spot (*Hypargos niveoguttatus*) which lives in the woods of Kenya, Mozambique and eastern Angola, will breed quickly if accommodated in a quiet, richly planted aviary

The Green Twin-spot (*Mandingoa nitidula*) was bred for the first time in captivity in 1960 in Germany

During the last few years, the Java Magpie from the *Spermestes* genus has become much sought after because it breeds quickly

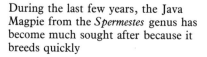

Left The Pagodah Mynah (*Sturnus pagodarum*) comes from Afghanistan, Sri Lanka and India. It needs a lot of space. In small cages it quickly becomes too fat. It sings most beautifully and will easily breed in a breeding box for starlings

Right The Black-headed Parrot (*Pionites melanocephala*), from South America, with good care it quickly becomes tame and will learn to speak a few words.

winged creature, drawn into stone'. The remarkable likeness between this bird and early flying reptiles (saurians) can be seen in four limestone fossils found in Bavaria. Its anatomy was very much like a saurian, but externally it looked much more like a bird because it possessed feathers. Close examination of its skeleton reveals a remarkable likeness between its feet and those of the little *Ornitholestes* dinosaur. The fact that the hind feet of both animals were talon-like suggests a similar lifestyle. They climbed onto branches of trees and bushes and from there, like parachutists, started their simple gliding flights.

The very first flights took place from above to below. The long midbone in the foot also suggests that the bird was capable of big strong jumps. We can assume that the primitive bird lived in mountainous areas among bushes and rocks. The most important ingredient of this habitat was, of course, water in the form of inland lakes where many types of animals lived. The fact that it had pointed teeth suggests that the primitive bird was a bird of prey, although it probably lived on the abundant supply of insects available to it. Birds became toothless rather late in the history of life on earth.

Little is known about the colour of their feathers. It is popularly assumed that they were white or red-brown. Similarly, there is no evidence of the sorts of

19

Above right Shama Thrush (*Turdus* or
Zoothera citrina). A ground bird from
Asia, Thailand and Moluccan Islands,
which will breed quickly

Right A pair of Fire Finches (*Lagonosticta
senegala*) can be kept well in a mixed
collection

Below The Toucan (*Ramphastos
sulfuratus*) lives in South-east Guatemala,
South Mexico and Honduras. It is 50cm
(18in) long and in captivity can become
extremely tame.

The Goldfinch (*Carduelis carduelis*) is one of the five aviary and cage birds which are suited for breeding with canaries. The goldfinch in this country nests in gardens, parks and orchards

nests built by the birds or the appearance of their eggs. Because *Archaeopteryx* is more bird-like than reptile-like, it is assumed that the eggs had hard shells.

There are a multitude of unanswered questions regarding the evolution of birds. Unfortunately their fragile bones are poorly preserved as fossils. When a bird died, its remains were usually scattered by other creatures living off carrion. To increase their powers of flight by weight reduction Avian bones are light and hollow and so disintegrate fairly quickly. The petrification process or the formation of imprints in stone takes centuries. A bird skeleton seldom had enough time to turn into stone before it decomposed completely. From the Cretaceous period to the present time – an enormous period of time of approximately 65 million years – there are no fossil remains of land birds which might enable the reconstruction of these creatures. Only a few examples of waterbirds from this period have been found including a very lean duck-like bird and *Ichthyornis victor*, a little wading bird. The former is one of the few aquatic birds from the Cretaceous period of which reconstructions could be made. It must have been an excellent flier with strong, well-developed wings. Its flying muscles were extremely well-developed, as was the large ridge on its

21

Right The Rainbow Bunting (*Passerina leclancherii*) originates from West Mexico. The female is plainer than the male. Despite its conspicuous colours these birds know how to hide themselves well in bushes. They make ideal cage birds

Below The Red-headed Starling (*Amblycerus holosericus*) from South America, Argentine and Paraguay lives in muddy regions and feeds mainly on insects.

breastbone to which the flight muscles were attached. It had to move its wings constantly in flight, that is, it could fly only actively. But this also meant that its flight ability was continuously developing. *Ichthyornis victor* had nearly the same characteristics. Its head was rather big, its beak enormous and it had little sharp conical teeth. Whether it had smaller or bigger swimming membranes than the present-day duck is not known. It represented the typical intermediate form of the aquatic bird. The tarsal bone of its feet was shorter than the shin bone (tibiatarsus) with its foot skeleton's position and development having more likeness to a wading foot rather than a swimming foot. It is often assumed that pre-historic animals looked like monsters, but *Ichthyornis victor* had nothing monster-like about it. It was no more than 20-25cm (8-10in) high and its body length measured about 14cm (6in). One could have kept it in a birdhouse! But it was a different matter with *Hesperornis regalis*, an ancestral diving bird which was 2m (6ft) long. The wingstumps of *Hesperornis regalis* are relatively smaller than the ones of birds living today. It had sharp conical teeth with which it must have hunted fishes and cuttle-fish. The big sea-divers of today are assumed to be direct descendants of *Hesperornis regalis*.

From this general look at the origin of a few bird types we can see how some living birds might have arrived at their present-day form and function. But, as mentioned earlier, the fossil record for most birds is very poor and when we look around the world at all the differently-adapted kinds, we can do no more than wonder at the stages through which their ancestors might have passed. Evolution is a slow process and, of course, in the birds that we know, it is still happening today. If changes are occurring in the birds that we know, it is impossible for us to detect them. All we can do is observe and wonder at their adaptations which seem so 'fixed', as though they have been in existence for millions of years. Among some examples of bird specialists are swifts which are renowned fliers and have completely developed wings, but helpless feet. Ducks and geese, which are also good fliers, possess strong breast muscles and firm leg-combs. Swans, excellent swimmers and fliers, can move only with difficulty on land on their relatively weak feet. Chickens have strong legs and are slowly losing their flying ability. Pheasants, quails and other poultry will suffer the same fate. Many wading-birds move around on long legs enabling them to wade far into the water in search of food without getting their plumage wet. Other clear forms of adaptation to environment and food are to be seen in beak forms, feathers, nest construction, development of chicks and the fact that there are birds of passage, resident birds and migratory birds. Life is far too short to see the changes in the evolution process, but those who are aware that this is going on, will no doubt continue to discover exciting aspects of ornithology.

The development of birds to the forms which we now know took place during the Tertiary period which lasted from 60 million years ago until 1 million years ago. The climax of this progress took place during Pliocene phase at the end of the Tertiary period.

The living bird

The plumage is the bird's most distinctive feature which, as already mentioned, was derived in the course of evolution from the scales of reptiles. Feathers are extremely fine creations of horn which protect the body. There are several kinds of feather, each modified to serve a special use. The downy feathers conserve body heat and the top feathers smooth the birds body contours into a streamlined shape. These contour feathers are distributed in well-defined feathertracts. In some species, like the woodpecker, tail feathers developed into means of support. The colour of feathers is determined by either the pigment in the feather or the microscopic structure of the feather. Common pigments are the melanins, ranging from yellow-brown to black, and the lipochromes, ranging from yellow to red. Blue and other brilliant colours are the result of certain feather structures. The fact that rib-cage and lumbar vertebrae are one unit is of great importance because the very important flight muscles are attached to it, as is the high breastbone comb. In the wings we clearly recognise the forelimbs of their ancestors, the reptiles. In many birds, the breast muscles may be as much as 15-20 per cent of their total weight. There are many neck vertebrae, making the neck long and flexible, resulting from the fact that head and beak had to take over the function of the earlier front legs as the wings were developing. The bill manipulates food and nest material, feeds the young and is a weapon against attackers. The high body temperature (about 41°C or 104°F) is maintained by an efficient heart and circulatory system which, like the respiratory system, shows special adaptation. The rather small lungs connect with various air-sacs which make the bird's system of breathing a very effective one. Furthermore these air-sacs take care of warmth, insulation and weight reduction. As a result of the high energy consumption, the bird's need for nourishment is great. Most birds have extremely good eyesight, with a visual acuity of 6 to 8 times that of man. Most of them are dependent upon their eyes for finding their food, for detecting predators and for recognizing their mates. An exception to this rule, from New Zealand, is the nocturnal Kiwi which has

The Yellow-naped Yuhina (*Yuhina flavicollis*) from South-east Asia is not unsuitable as an indoor bird. However, during the summer months it should be housed in an aviary. The bird sings beautifully and not too loudly

reduced and rather short-sighted eyes. As a compensation it has well-developed hearing and smelling ability.

Distribution

Because of their ability to adapt, birds spread all over the world. With continuous adjustments new species were created and old ones became extinct. This development still takes place today. Again and again birds adapt to new circumstances and if they do not succeed they are condemned to extinction. The greatest numbers and species of birds are found in tropical or sub-tropical areas.

The habitat of most species is limited to certain geographical areas: tanagers and humming birds are found only in North and South America (Neotropical fauna); Mouse-birds are found only in Africa, south of the Sahara (Ethiopic fauna); by far the greatest number of pheasant and babbler species occurs in South-east Asia (Oriental fauna); Emu and Birds of Paradise are typical representatives of the Australasian fauna. Closer to home, the Dunnock has its habitat in the palearctic fauna, i.e. Europe, Asia up to the Himalayas and North

Left The Yolk-yellow Weaver (*Sitagra vitellina*) lives in Senegal, North Tanzania and along the Red Sea. It is a strong, very active bird, which can be kept easily in an outdoor aviary, even throughout the winter

Right The Indian White-eye (*Zosterops palpebrosa*) from India and Indochina belongs to a very big family which has about a hundred different members. They are agile warbler-like birds, which stay mainly in bushes where they look for insects. They also feed on berries, buds and nectar. In a cage they will eat a honey-mixture, orange slices, pieces of hard-boiled eggs, cheese and bread soaked in milk

Africa. This demonstrates that it is rare for one species to spread over a large part of the world. The exceptions are a few species of water-based birds and some birds of prey.

The reason that sparrows and starlings can today be found in Australia and in northern USA is that they were imported from Europe in the 19th Century. All birds are adapted to their environments and they cannot live successfully in those which are different, a fact which a bird-keeper must never lose sight of. Thus, there are limits to their range of distribution. Keeping and breeding birds successfully can be achieved only if they are given good care and environments (i.e. suitable birdhouses) where their natural habitats are re-created as best as possible with the right food and appropriate cage companions. If we do not comply with these requirements, birds in birdhouses will suffer the same problems as their companions outside. As a result of many landscape changes believed by man to be necessary, bird numbers have declined. Birds have become so-called culture-escapists. By luck, it also happens sometimes that birds adapt to new situations and thus become culture-followers. But the question must be asked whether such changes will, sooner or later, have a detrimental effect on the number of species around today.

Below left Birds in a cherry tree by Wang Ch'eng P'ei (approximately AD 1725-1805), Museum of East-Asian Art, Cologne

Below centre The wild canary (*Serinus canaria*) is the ancestor of all canaries. It was bred in Spain as early as the 15th century

Below right There are four different kinds of Hooded Lory (*Eos squamata*) in the Indian sub-continent

2 Aviculture for everyone

It is not known where birds were first kept in captivity, but it must have been long before man could express himself in wall paintings or writing on parchment. There is evidence in the cultural history of both the old and new world to indicate that birds were kept by many different races. Paintings and hieroglyphics left behind by Ancient Egyptians contain many references to doves, parrots, ducks and ibises as well as other birds used for hunting ducks, snipes and herons.

Silk paintings, vases and other ceramic objects of the Ancient Chinese portray a rich collection of colourful birds. If the illustrations are to be interpreted correctly, most of the birds shown were domesticated. It is assumed that the history of the chicken goes back at least 5000 years to the first township in India. The chicken, descended from the Red Jungle Fowl (*Gallus gallus*) which still lives in the bamboo forests of South-east Asia, was carried by man to all parts of the world. Today more than 200 different breeds are known, from the Bantam to the most beautiful Onagodori, a Japanese chicken with a fantastic tail, often several metres in length.

The Incas in South America also took an interest in birds and even tamed some species, such as the Amazon Parrot, which they kept in their houses and

Old illustrations show that birds were kept as domestic animals early in history. Here, a goose, Egyptian drawing 2750 BC, 4th Dynasty, Egyptian Museum, Cairo

temples. Therefore we can assume that birds are some of the oldest domesticated animals. Over the centuries, the practice of keeping and caring for birds grew. But the reasons for keeping them changed continually. For instance, hawks and falcons were used to capture other birds and small mammals. Falconry is a sport that has been known for many centuries.

When nomadic people gradually settled, they had more time at their disposal for wall paintings and carvings which often depicted courageous deeds carried out during hunting. Drawings of various birds still exist from this period. When man discovered that some birds also provide food, falcons and other hunting birds became less popular, and instead the breeding of chickens began. Today the chicken provides one of the cheapest forms of meat. In the USA each year, nearly two billion slaughter-chickens are produced. The number of laying-hens in America alone is nearly twice as many as the world's human population: nearly 640 million eggs are sold yearly. Selective breeding has also increased egg-yield. A hen at the time of Roman civilisation laid 50 to 60 eggs a year, whereas today the world-record for eggs laid by one hen in a year is 361.

In the Near East, the pigeon must have established itself as a common garden or park bird in ancient times. Today the total number of pigeons cannot even be estimated. The pigeon has been used for various purposes for thousands of

Right A romantic dove-cage on a gutter in Indonesia. In ancient times, the dove must have been a common garden and park bird in eastern countries. Later it spread throughout the whole world

Below The God Horus in form of a falcon, imprinted on a relief of the Egyptian King Wadji, approximately 2900 BC, Louvre, Paris

The 'Goldfinch' by Carel Fabritius
(1622-1654) which he painted in his last
year of life. Mauritshaus, The Hague

Wild Budgerigars (*Melopsittacus
undulatus*) in Australia

years: messenger services, food and decoration, and pigeon-racing has become a world-wide sport.

However, they have become a major nuisance in most of the world's larger cities. Their excreta is a constant threat to public health and it also does great damage to buildings. But it is not only the pigeon that has become distributed in such great numbers over the whole world. The millions of canaries kept in cages and aviaries are more numerous than the entire stock of wild canaries in the Canary Islands, from where European seamen first brought this bird in the 15th century.

The close relationship between man and birds has existed throughout history. There are a number of incidents recorded in the bible which illustrate the roles of birds as friends or companions to man. The dove has always been a symbol of peace. In ancient Egypt, much care was lavished on various water birds, which were kept in specially constructed ponds, particularly in the nobility's large gardens or close to their temples. There is a statue of the God Horus of Shahom, which has the shape of a falcon and stands as a massive monument among the columns of Edfu. The Egyptians also built huge bird-cages in the large houses of the rich which were filled with numerous songbirds and parrots. Pigeons were already kept at that time. In earlier times, the nobility and members of the higher Indian castes possessed aviaries where they bred not only songbirds, but also different kinds of parrots and parakeets. Some birds were even regarded as having priceless value and a man was appointed exclusively to look after them. We also know that the old Egyptians brought parakeets from India with the intention of breeding them in specially constructed birdhouses. Some years later, Alexander the Great brought the first Rose-ringed Parakeets to Europe after seeing them on his travels through India. In the Middle Ages, monks kept caged birds not only to study their behaviour but also to sell them to royalty. From thereon the hobby of aviculture gradually developed in Europe. In the 15th and 16th centuries, both rich and poor started to keep many species of native songbirds.

The best known songbird is probably the canary which the Spaniards were already breeding in the 15th century. The Budgerigar is a relatively new cage bird, introduced to England in 1840 by the bird artist, John Gould and a few years later on the Continent. Much has happened to this small parrot since then and a description of its development in becoming one of the best loved species in cages and aviaries would fill a voluminous book.

During the days when European seamen crossed the seas in huge sailing vessels, they would often bring birds back with them as presents for their wives and children, amongst the most popular of which were parrots and parakeets from South America, where they had been domesticated some centuries earlier.

A chat between two green Budgerigars (*Melopsittacus undulatus*). Budgerigars are companionable birds by nature

A bird show

Dwarf Parrots of the *Forpus* genus. Here is a pair of Green Dwarf Parrots (*Forpus passerinus*) from South America

The Diamond Dove (*Geopelia cuneata*), here a silver-grey mutation, originates from Australia. The bird can pass the winter in a sunny outdoor aviary

In the ancient empires of China and Japan, quite a number of hard- and softbills were kept in the cages and aviaries of palaces. Rich collections of waterbirds are shown on many silk paintings as well as being delicately carved in wood and ivory. These are the countries of origin for many birds now kept by aviculturists. An example is *Lonchura domestica*. During its period of domestication (which can be traced back to about 1700) different varieties were bred and it finally became a very popular ornamental bird. It came quite late to Europe: to England 1860, to Germany 1872 and to Holland 1874.

On its arrival, it quickly gained wide acceptance amongst bird-breeders.

One of the last species to become completely domesticated was the well-known Zebra Finch of Australia. We propose to look at some of its many illustrious domesticated predecessors in Chapter 5.

Aviculturists often find themselves having to justify the practice of keeping birds in captivity, especially to members of animal protection societies. Critics maintain that caged birds are deprived of their freedom and are dependent on the goodwill of their owners, and that the birds' welfare is therefore subject to human whims and degrees of efficiency and benevolence.

It is undeniable that in the past birds which would have been better off left in the wild were kept in captivity, and that cruel practices occurred for the amusement of birdowners. Present day bird enthusiasts should therefore try to

Head study of a Common Crown Dove

(*Goura cristata cristata*) a native of New Guinea. In the past these birds were hunted, but today they are protected. They were easy prey for the hunter because of their size

Lonchura domestica breed best if they are a single pair of their kind in the aviary. If there are further *Lonchura domestica* they inspect each other's nests and breeding seems to fall by the wayside. There are pure white, beige-white and brown-spotted variations

understand the arguments of people who are opposed to the caging of birds. Both are motivated by the same feelings, a love of nature in general and birds in particular.

Nowadays aviculturists play an important role in the conservation of bird species. With increasing pollution, de-forestation, and the drainage of swamps, ponds, rivers and lakes, the environment is being slowly destroyed, with little consideration for the many forms of life which are thus threatened with extinction. It is thanks to the zoos that many species have been saved from dying out, and thanks to the aviculturists that many birds have been preserved for future generations.

Sympathy for caged animals is entirely misplaced. The great number of nests full of chicks which appear every year in aviaries show that aviary birds cannot be suffering unduly from being in captivity. They have many enemies and predators in the wild, human beings included, and their natural habitats are slowly being encroached upon by civilization. Naturalists have studied how birds which at one time were found only in the forests have moved to parks and later into towns. Some species totally vanish from sight if they are not able to move on when their habitat is encroached upon.

Top right Saffron Finch (*Sicalis flaveola*) from South America is often agressive towards smaller birds in the aviary. Therefore it is better housed together with bigger finches. The female is not quite so impetuous as the male

Centre right Black-cheeked Love Bird (*Agapornis personata nigrigensis*) was discovered in 1906 in North-west Rhodesia by Dr W. L. Scater and introduced to the public for the first time in the Berliner Tiergarten in 1908

Right The Gouldian Finch (*Chloebia gouldiae*) from tropical North Australia is a cave inhabitant in the wild often building its nest in a termites' hill. It is a valuable bird

Above The Nonpareil Bunting (*Passerina ciris*) is extremely colourful

Left Green Twin-spot (*Mandingoa nitidula*)

Centre left The Doublebar Finch (*Poephila bichenovii*) take some time to acclimatize before they can be kept in an aviary

Above A judge at work in a bird-show, examining exhibits of colour canaries. He tries to look at birds from different positions to see the colours better. Then he will take them out of their cages to check the colour of the wingquills and to ensure that no quills are missing

Left The number of quills in the tail feathers must be correct. At a showing of posture canaries special attention is given to the shape and carriage of the bird. These have to live up to the standards set by the show committee

Right A Parrot-finch (*Erythrura psittacea*)

At a show, experiences can be compared
and discussed

For many centuries, man has kept domesticated animals, including birds; not only to provide food but also for the aesthetic pleasure they provide.

Included amongst the birds which have long been domesticated are geese, ducks, chickens, guinea-fowl, turkeys and pigeons. Canaries, Budgerigars and Bengalese and Zebra Finches have been kept in captivity slightly less long. Other species in the process of becoming domesticated are Agapornis, parakeets and other finches.

To believe that birds suffer untold anguish when confined in a cage or aviary is to 'humanize' them; human beings suffer in captivity because behind bars or barbed wire they imagine how beautiful freedom would be; but such imagination is only possessed by humans. Animals live mainly for the present, are happy and satisfied if they have enough to eat and drink, sufficient light, plenty of room to move and exercise, opportunity to reproduce and protection from their enemies and bad weather. An escaped bird will often return to its cage of its own accord. Many people think that a bird would fly away jubilantly if its cage door were opened, but in fact the bird would probably feel rather bewildered, unsure and inhibited.

Provided that birds are properly cared for, there should be no criticism of keeping them in cages and aviaries. The majority of owners lavish care and attention on their birds, go out of their way to provide them with the most appropriate food; and so create a little piece of nature where birds can build their nests without restraint or disturbance, and rear their young with a ready supply of food.

Multicoloured Finch (*Passerina versicolor*) which comes from Texas. It is a prolific and amicable bird in a mixed collection. When migration time comes in the Autumn, it gets restless and tends to fly against the roof of the aviary which can result in grave injuries. To avoid this happening, it is advisable to shield the roof with a piece of jute

Opposite page Cut-throat Finch (*Amadina fasciata*) comes from Africa and is known as a nest-destroyer

3 Choosing the right bird

The purchase of a bird requires careful planning as a sensible choice is an important factor in the ultimate enjoyment of the bird. It may be unwise to buy a lively or colourful bird that catches your fancy without having thought about its needs. Rather you should take your time and remember the different characteristics of different species. If, for example, you are interested in sensitive tropical or sub-tropical birds, it is wise only to buy these when the temperature for acclimatization is favourable, i.e. from late spring through to early autumn.

The bird in the shop-window may have been through a lot before it reached its destination. This is especially true of imported birds which have long and hazardous journeys behind them, often having been packed into tiny cages with hundreds of others. They have to get used to different food and climate. The thoughtful bird-dealer will make sure that his new birds have a few quiet days before he puts them in a cage for sale, so that they have some time for adjustment.

The purchase of a bird is and remains a matter of experience. It is wise to have a look at several bird-dealers before making a decision. Birds which sit with

Left The Red Canary was bred for the first time in 1872 and was exhibited in the same year by its breeder, W. A. Blakeston, at Crystal Palace in London

Right Young interest at a canary show

Birdmarket at Noordermart in Amsterdam. Nowadays birdmarkets are to be found almost every week in Holland and Belgium. Before you decide on buying, you should examine the bird very carefully

fluffed-up feathers should not be bought because this is an indication that they are not fully fit. Always observe birds from a distance initially because if you get too near the cage they will fly about excitedly. If a bird is healthy, its feathers should lay flush and tight to its body. It should look around observantly and react to the behaviour of other birds. All in all, it should make a fresh and lively impression. If you approach it closely, it should try to escape. If it remains still, it is a sign of illness rather than tameness. An active bird, once it gets used to surroundings and care, will become very tame.

Before you decide on your purchase take the bird in your hands. If you do not feel confident enough at first ask the bird-dealer to do so. In any case check its condition. To do this properly, hold the bird in such a way that its back lies in your hand and use your thumb and index finger to check its breast. If the breastbone sticks out sharply, the bird is too thin and its muscular system insufficient. It would not be a good bird to buy.

A healthy bird has well-developed muscles on both sides of its sternum and only a small edge of the sternum comb can be felt. Check whether feathers around the vent are dirty because this is a sign of diarrhoea which is difficult to cure. If you find this, do not proceed further with the purchase. However, note that if you take a newly imported and untamed bird into your hand, it will pass a watery secretion out of fright. This is a normal reaction and has nothing to do with diarrhoea or intestinal troubles. Once the bird is used to its new environment, it will become lively. Neither should you worry if the bird has one or several feathers missing, for example, on its wings or tail. Flying about in cages which are too small and being frequently handled can impair the plumage; but, with good care, it will recover.

The first few days
Your new acquisition should be put into quarantine in a spacious cage for two weeks in a place which has sufficient light but no draughts. Offer the same food as the bird-dealer and supplement this with other food which is suitable for that particular type of bird. The feeds that bird-dealers provide are, unfortunately often limited to seed mixtures or certain universal feeds with little variety. It is therefore essential that the aviculturist should know right from the start which food is needed by which bird.

A bird cannot be without food for more than 24 hours. Therefore only buy birds which can get to their final destination within a few hours. The shorter the journey the better for the bird. if you cannot accommodate the new arrival before evening, leave the lights on for a few hours to give the bird opportunity to

Canaries, *Lonchura domestica* and Zebra Finches are for sale in the market

45

Top right A potential buyer checks whether the breast of the canary might be red or purple or puffed up (inflated). Such birds cannot be used for breeding. Also, overlong claws on the male can hinder copulation. A female with overlong claws might damage its eggs. A bird which suffers from diarrhoea should not be bought because it is difficult to cure

Centre These are mainly lutino Budgerigars

Right The Superb Parrot (*Polytelis swainsonii*) from Australia is best kept in pairs in a spacious birdcage. During winter it is recommended to house this bird in an unheated room

eat and drink. Do not leave the bird in the dark. Give it enough light to adjust to its surroundings. Otherwise it might flutter about restlessly and bump into obstacles, resulting in serious injuries.

Food should be sprinkled at the bottom of the cage as well as being put into feeding pots. Many birds will not be used to feed and drink from dishes and will instinctively search for food on the floor. It is not uncommon for birds to die of hunger because there was no food strewn on the floor, even though the necessary supplies were right in front of their beaks.

Examine the excreta carefully for the first few days. It must not be too watery. If this is the case, it is advisable to house the bird in warmer surroundings with a temperature of 30-35°C (86-95°F). But do not treat it as if it were sick. Just give it stale, white, milk-soaked bread and a few drops of Protovita in its drinking water. If it is a fruit-eating bird, put some honey on the bread. Once it looks completely healthy again, it can be returned to a more spacious cage, preferably on a sunny and warm morning when it has a chance of familiarising itself with its new environment and finding food and water.

I know of birds which have travelled through the whole of Europe from one owner to the next, because they are no good to anyone. It is important to have

The Turquoise Parakeet (*Neophema pulchella*) from Australia occurs in central Queensland, New South Wales and up to the border of Victoria. There it lives in pairs or in groups. It becomes active only at dawn. This bird was discovered in 1788. This precious genus will breed quickly in a spacious outdoor aviary

precise details about the bird for your own sake and that of a future buyer. Ask for a birth register if you buy a bird.

When buying big parakeets, cockatoos or parrots, take care that they do not have bald patches. If this is the case, you can almost be certain that they are feather-pluckers; a habit which is difficult to eradicate and, in some cases, is even hereditary. Another group of fruit-eating, tropical birds like the tanagers, Mynahs and leafbirds often have sticky fruit-pieces around the bill which hinder the growth of feathers and result in bald patches. But this is no reason to refrain from buying. With good care, quick recovery is guaranteed. These birds have probably been given pieces of fruit which were too big for them, by the bird-dealer or during transport. Insufficient opportunity for bathing and warm temperatures make the fruit remnants sticky. Fruit ought to be cut very finely.

Hardbills, tropical and sub-tropical birds should have a glossy plumage, clear eyes, healthy feet with claws not too long and a well-formed and well-closing beak. The head should not appear thin.

Suitable birds
Now we come to the question of which kind of bird you should keep. You have to decide whether you just want one bird in a cage in the living-room or study or

Left The Scarlet Tanager (*Ramphocelus bresilius*) from South-east Brazil. To retain its colour this bird needs a good insectile mixture together with soya bean flour. Furthermore its feeds should include black and red berries, soaked raisins and sultanas, chopped dates, insect and ant chrysalis. The hen is reddish brown and it lays about 3-4 eggs which it hatches in 12 days

Right The Cockatiel (*Nymphicus hollandicus*) from Australia is already such a domesticated bird that, alongside several other colours, white mutations can be bred

Above The Common Mynah
(*Acridotheres tristis*) lives in Indochina and
Afghanistan. It quickly becomes tame
and learns to imitate tunes

Golden-fronted Fruitsucker (*Chloropsis
aurifrons*) originates from the Himalayan
region and is also a good imitator. It has a
lovely song and can be kept with other
species

The Yellow-rumped Seed-eater or
Black-throated Canary (*Serinus
atrogularis*) from Africa sings like a lark
and despite its plain plumage makes a
good bird for a mixed collection, because
it gets on well with other birds. Male and
female are difficult to distinguish. The
female is rather quiet. It is well suited for
breeding

Above Dilute Pastel Canary

Left The White Canary. Both stem from the wild canary (*Serinus canaria*) which has its home in the Canary Islands

The Virginian Cardinal (*Richmondena cardinalis*) is also called the Virginian Nightingale because of its powerful song

Below The male Indigo Bunting (*Passerina cyanea*) from America loses its beautiful colour in autumn and becomes grey-brown like the hen

The Pied Mynah (*Sturnus or Sturnopastor contra*) originates from Bali and Java. It is a most agile bird which deserves its reputation as a singer. The female has a smaller head than the male

maybe you want a bird-room or even a birdhouse. Do you have a big enough garden? Do you want birds for their song, their colours or their behaviour? You must also ask yourself if you intend breeding them.

If you are a beginner, it is wise to start with species which are straightforward to care for and which breed easily, Australian parakeets provide a good starting point. A pair of Cockatiels or Bourke's Parakeets would give you some experience and later on you can try more difficult species. This way, it will not cost you a fortune as you can sell the resulting offspring in order to add to your collection with, for example, Song-Parakeets or Turquoise Grass Parakeets. Make sure you buy only young specimens. In addition, reserve the right to change the birds if they do not form a pair. Beware of extremely low prices because there will probably be some kind of handicap such as the bird not wishing or not being able to breed or being too aggressive. Good birds are not cheap, so beware of special offers.

Strangely enough, the possession of a single caged bird is still the most common practice. Mostly they are those which have lovely songs (canaries), or talk (Mynahs, parrots) or possess brilliant colours (various tropical kinds). Among the canaries, the Roller and Border are the best known in living-rooms

The Munia (*Lonchura domestica*)

Below The Waxbill (*Estrilda troglodytes*) from Central Africa

Above African Silverbill (*Euodice malabarica cantans*) from North Africa

Right Recently developed crest mutation of the Zebra Finch (*Taeniopygia guttata*)

along with the Yellow Canary. Many people think a canary just has to be yellow. A Roller does not have such impressive plumage, but makes up for it with its melodic song. If you want a yellow canary, which also sings beautifully, go for the slightly cheaper Yellow Roller. Those canaries, bred for their colour, can be quite beautiful and males do have quite a nice song. But when bred, colour is more important than song. Colours range from Dilute Green, Cinnamon Dilute, Melanin, Red, Lemon-Yellow to Blue. If you visit a canary-show, you will be amazed at the variety of colours. Borders are mostly yellow. Although their song is worth listening to, it sounds 'tinnier' than that of the Rollers.

The hardbill Grey Singing Finch is also recommended because it is easy to keep. It sings beautifully and becomes tame in no time at all. This also applies to the cheerful Green Singing Finch which has a lovely plumage and song. Slightly more expensive, but very lovely and tame is the Pekin Robin with melodious song and colourful plumage. The Indigo Bunting also has these two qualities to a high degree. Both species need to be housed in a big cage, for example in a spacious budgerigar-cage. They regularly need insect food, meal-worms and good lean universal food.

Rather more expensive and more unusual are the different tropical starlings

The Orange-cheeked Waxbill (*Estrilda melpoda*) is not a bad singer. Once acclimatized and receiving insects this bird will go to breed in a well planted aviary in a closed or half-closed nesting box. The outdoor birdhouse should be somewhat sheltered

such as the Shama (*Copsychus malabaricus*), the Cardinals (especially the Virginian Cardinal) or the leafbirds (particularly the Golden-fronted Fruitsucker). They all have a very striking plumage and excellent song. If kept outdoors, the choice is almost unlimited. You have to remember, however, that not all birds will get on with each other. Some kinds become very aggressive towards others during the pairing and breeding season. You will quickly know which birds need to be separated from others. As a rule you ought to buy and house together only those birds which are of approximately the same size and require the same care.

For inside aviaries you can consider for example: all *Lonchura domestica* species, African Silverbills, Waxbills, Cordon Bleus or Orange-cheeked Waxbills. More expensive are astrilds, Australian Budgerigars and tanagers.

Not all species breed quickly. If the weather is favourable, you can soon expect a new generation of Zebra Finches. Neither do you have to wait long

A pair of Violet-eared Waxbills or Grenadiers (*Granatina granatina*). These birds occur in West and South Africa. They can only be kept well if they are given insects daily. They are difficult to keep and not suitable for beginners

with *Lonchura domestica* or African Silverbills. But this does not mean that, in every breeding season, you can expect numerous healthy chicks. You will always encounter individual birds which have problems among those species named, whereas other kinds might give birth to several splendid young ones quite unexpectedly. This makes the hobby such an interesting adventure.

Some success is guaranteed if you follow these tips: Do not start the breeding season with birds which are too young. For small birds this means a minimum age of 5 to 10 months or two years for bigger kinds. Therefore, it is important to know the origin, age and behaviour of your birds which can only be achieved by well-kept records. Equally important are good housing and suitable food mixtures. By good housing, is meant plenty of room for them to fly around in. If you lack room, you must restrict yourself to birds which do not require much room. A garden aviary is of course the best possible accommodation.

Once the birds are housed well, you must take good care of them. They require fresh bathing and drinking water daily as well as sufficient food. Sick birds should be separated immediately. The sand at the bottom of a cage should be renewed at least once a week. The aviary should be dug over at least every fortnight. However, do not do this during breeding time when you should leave the breeding pair undisturbed. Keep everything as clean as possible to avoid diseases. Do not give germs a chance – make sure that drinking dishes, bathing dishes, feeding dishes, sleeping places and perches are regularly cleaned and disinfected. If you do not have a minimum of one hour a day to devote to your birds, there is no point in taking up this hobby. Start off slowly. Begin with a few species which are cheap to buy. From the sale of their offspring you can gradually buy more valuable species.

One final point: Don't let your enthusiasm for your birds mean less time spent with your family. This is an ideal hobby for the family and a marvellous way to teach children about nature. Take your children to the aviary and explain the behaviour of the different birds. Let them hold nests, eggs and chicks. This is the best way to rear the nature-lovers that we badly need today.

4 Providing a suitable home

The immense variety of birds and their individual characteristics should be carefully considered when planning their housing. Parrots should not be put into canary boxes nor finches in parrot cages. Many different types of cages and aviaries have been developed over the years and it is not always easy to make the right choice, especially if you have only just taken up aviculture. However here are a few general guidelines for the responsible housing of pet birds.

Above all, you ought to ensure that cages and aviaries are of simple design so they can be cleaned easily. Ornamental models may be attractive, but they can be awkward to clean and so make excellent hiding places for parasites. Home-built cages and aviaries need to be painted with a safe paint, like the sort you would use for children's furniture. Caustic and creosote can also be used since they are both harmless, though the latter does tend to give off an unpleasant smell for a couple of days. If creosote has been used on an indoor-cage, allow a week before moving birds in, as the fumes of one of the ingredient oils can be

Left An outdoor cage with abundant plant-life inside as well as outside. It forms a piece of living nature whch integrates harmoniously with the whole garden

Right A modern glass canary-cage with gabled roof

Right A modern rectangular Budgerigar cage is easy to clean

Below Because they are so nosey, Budgerigars will amuse themselves a great deal of the time if toys are available. These toys should be made out of plastic so that they are easy to clean.

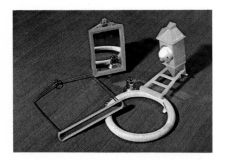

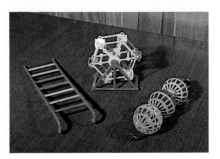

A bamboo cage. Not a bad ornament, but as housing for birds rather impractical and, above all, unhygienic

A modern wooden cage for 'Harzer' Roller

harmful to the birds in a closed room. In general, these paints are only suitable for outdoor aviaries.

Chromium-plated cages are put into acid baths before leaving the manufacturer and so any newly-bought cage should be washed down with warm water. Any newly-painted cage or aviary obviously needs to be completely dry before putting birds in.

Some cages have plastic-coated bars and are therefore unsuitable for parrots and parakeets who explore everything with their beaks. It could be very dangerous if they managed to swallow pieces of plastic. They could also escape fairly quickly if there was anything other than steel bars on the cage.

Cages

One of the most common forms of cage is the box-type cage which is rectangular and made of hard wood (Oak or Beech). This type of cage is closed on all sides except for the front. I know from experience that birds breed quickly and easily in these. You should avoid porous woods because these provide an ideal harbour for insect pests. Hard-board or plywood are both suitable and painted wood is easily kept clean. Any paint colour is suitable. I

A tower cage for a pair of tame Budgerigars. The horizontal bars give the Budgerigars an opportunity to climb

Above right The Blue Crown Lory (*Loriculus or Coryllis galgullus*) should be kept in pairs to avoid squabbles with other birds

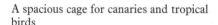

A spacious cage for canaries and tropical birds

prefer brown and green, but I know people who have painted their birdcages very colourfully. It is just a matter of taste. The important consideration for a cage is that it is solid and spacious with drink and food containers within easy reach. A cage with several little doors makes cleaning much easier.

For the weekly cleaning of cages, use warm water with a disinfectant which is harmless to the birds. After cleaning, rinse everything again with warm water. Wait until the cages are completely dry before you return the birds. You can speed up the drying process with a hairdrier or ventilator. This might be necessary if the birds are temporarily housed in small cages where they might get restless and even injure themselves.

Perches should be of different shapes and sizes in order to relax and strengthen the various muscles of the birds' feet and legs. Natural perching such as twigs of fruit-trees, Hazelbushes, Willows or Conifers may also be provided. But be careful not to use wood that easily splinters and could be dangerous to the birds. With perches of Oak, Maple, Sycamore or Lilac, take care to strip off the poisonous bark. Natural perching, even though it needs to be renewed from time to time, has the advantage of birds being able to gnaw on it, thus keeping their beaks in good condition and alleviating boredom.

Perches should be fixed securely and placed in such a way that the bird has sufficient room for flying exercises. The sudden collapse of a perch can cause panic. Do not place one perch directly over another. In this way you will avoid birds on top soiling the ones below with their droppings. For the same reason, keep the perches clear of drink, bathing or feeding vessels. When doing your weekly cleaning rub the perches with coarse rather than fine sandpaper, because birds find smooth perches difficult to grip.

There is a wide range of food and drink containers available in plastic, china or ceramic. Whatever type you use, make sure they are kept clean. If they get chipped, renew them because cracks provide ideal refuges for parasites.

The bottom of the cage should be covered with a layer of sand. Several suitable types of litter are available containing grit or other minerals which are essential to a bird's digestive system. Birds which eat fruit tend to have a rather fluid excreta. For such birds it is best to use firm wrapping paper rather than newspaper as floor covering and sprinkle a thin layer of sand on it. Daily renewal is recommended.

Outdoor aviaries
The design and construction of outdoor aviaries should be as simple as possible. Much depends on the space available but also on the kind of birds you wish to

Below Breeding Budgerigars indoors is easily possible. The birds quickly become tame

Left The Greenfinch (*Chloris chloris*) an indigenous bird, is ideally suited for hybridizing with canaries

Below Expensive outdoor birdhouses which are ideal for keeping and breeding *Platycercus*

Above The Splendid Parakeet (*Neophema splendida*) truly lives up to its name

Below Alexander Parakeet (*Psittacula eupatria nipalensis*) will normally nest in holes in trees, but, in a cage, it will also accept a closed breeding box

Above right View from living-room onto an outdoor aviary

Right The inside of an outdoor aviary. Because of the rich plant life birds will quickly feel at home and start breeding

Below A simple garden aviary

keep. Suitable building materials are bricks, timber, hardboard and iron rods. The roof can be of brick, slate, planed planks, asbestos or asphalt sheeting or corrugated plastic which is highly recommended because it allows in light. Constructions entirely of timber are not advisable for Budgerigars or other parakeets because they are born whittlers and break a lot off with their beaks.

The floor should be concrete, to prevent vermin getting into the aviary. Even better, bury glass fragments and wire netting into the concrete. Concrete by itself is not enough of a barrier for unwanted marauders.

Sufficient numbers of perches should be installed to avoid fighting over seating and roosting places. Plants and bushes make the best and most natural roosting places. Suitable vegetation for this are Red-currant, Beech, Privet, *Spirea*, Mountain-ash, Buckthorn, Wild Cherry, Birch, Gorse and Hip. Ivy, *Cotoneaster*, *Mohonia*, Conifer and Box provide the most suitable vegetation for natural nesting places. Rhododendrons are suitable only for aviaries which do not house parakeets, because the leaves are poisonous.

The aviary itself is best integrated into the garden by being placed among trees and shrubs rather than looking forlorn and naked in the middle of the

The Little Sulphur-crested Cockatoo (*Cacatua sulphurea*) from Indonesia is a gregarious funny bird which quickly becomes tame and friendly towards children. Although it is frequently kept on a perch, a spacious birdhouse would be better

garden. It should be erected facing south. If this is impossible, it is better to have it south-east facing than south-west. Drinking and food vessels should be of the right sizes according to your birds, such as little ones for display finches and bigger ones for fruit-feeders, tits and parakeets. The same applies to the bathing vessels which should not be too deep. If you have one with a depth of 10cm (4in) or more, put a stone in the bottom. It is best to use a flat stone to enable the birds to climb onto it if they want to. If you make a little pond, the edges should have a very gradual slope and the pond's depth should not be more than 7cm (2¾in). Small feeding vessels must be firmly fixed to avoid birds overturning them.

If you keep quails, pheasants or other ground birds, it is important that the floor is well loosened up so that water can quickly drain away. On a concrete floor a thick layer of sawdust or coarse peat should be put down. Nothing is more dangerous to a bird than to walk and sleep on moist ground. You can avoid a lot of problems if you fix a number of strong perches approximately 50cm (20in) above the ground.

Whatever kinds of birds you keep in an aviary, make sure they have plenty of shrubbery such as Gorse, Scottish Heather or Elder. Above these bushes ensure the birdhouse is protected from downpours which can destroy nests, eggs or young. We also recommend providing a wide choice of nest boxes in the aviary (at least twice as many as there are pairs). If you build these boxes yourself, you can use plywood. During breeding time in the aviary small tropical birds tend to be rather shy, thus absolute peace and quiet is necessary.

1.5cm (½in) hexagonally-meshed wire netting is commonly used because squarely-welded wire netting is not so easy to stretch. The latter tends to be used for large parakeets, pheasants etc., with gauges of 1.25, 1.47 or 1.65mm (.05, .06 or .07in). It is recommended to paint this netting with green creosote.

Sometimes a bird-fancier has the rare opportunity of planning the erection of an aviary together with the building of his house. The best combination is to have the aviary as an extension of a room with the two being separated by glass, with a door in the glass-wall. You can then gain entrance into the aviary. This arrangement enables observation of the birds from the living room or study even though the birds are housed outside. The birds will become accustomed to this close human contact and will lose their initial apprehension quite quickly. Don't forget that in the evenings they should be protected from electric light.

5 Care and breeding of your birds

It is not difficult to buy birds, neither is it difficult to keep them healthy and cheerful if you follow the few basic rules. In the previous chapter we pointed out what to observe when you make your purchase. Once you have the birds at home, it is important to give newly-imported individuals the opportunity to acclimatise. How do we go about this? Let us look at a pair of Cordon Bleus. These are rather sensitive birds and many perish on their journey from Africa to Europe. The remaining ones go to a bird-dealer to begin with. Even though they might look pretty bad at this stage, these birds will be physically quite strong, otherwise they would not have survived the journey. A pair of Cordon Bleus (*Uraeginthus bengalus*) would normally be kept by a bird-dealer for a few months before being offered for sale in a pet-shop.

Well-cared-for birds should be colourful and healthy and if this is not the case, it is inadvisable to buy them. However, if you want to buy them anyway, you should help them to recuperate as follows. Take the pair home and put

Left A sub-species of the well known Blue Mountain Lorikeet from eastern Australia is the Mitchell's Lorikeet (*Trichoglossus haematod mitchelii*)

Right The Grey Cardinal (*Paroaria coronata*)

The Cordon Bleu (*Uraeginthus bengalus*) lives in an area bounded by Senegal to the Red Sea and south to Rhodesia. If the bird gets plenty of insects it will breed quickly in a spacious birdhouse. It is susceptible to cold and draught and it is recommended to offer them warm surroundings during winter

them in a room where they can have a good rest. Feed the new-comers with a wide choice of food, both plant and animal. Separate males and females in order for them to rest and recuperate from their various journeys and the changes in air and climate. Once the birds' plumage looks healthy, put them back together again but, in order to avoid them pairing, do not provide them with a nest box or nesting material. Don't forget to provide them with bathing water of room-temperature, an earthenware vessel containing washing sand, cuttle fishbone and charcoal. In view of the big change they are undergoing, it is extremely important to offer a varied choice of food so that they can adapt quickly to their new environment, change in diet and way of life.

In the open, birds search for their own varied forms of nourishment. They are their own doctors and they not only look after themselves but also their young ones. But things are very different in the cage or aviary where their keeper provides them with food, quite unlike that which they find in the wild. Therefore you have to try to get as close as possible to their natural foodstuffs. Acclimatisation also includes getting them accustomed to feeding from dishes and you should soak the various seeds before offering them to the birds. You

Right The Emerald-spotted Zebra Finch
(*Taeniopygia guttata*) originated from the
Australian Zebra Finch. It was one of the
last birds to be completely domesticated.
It breeds in cages as well as in aviaries.
The Emerald-spotted Zebra Finch was
bred for the first time in Denmark

The Lutino Budgerigar is the albino form
of all yellow and green colour mutations.
It was bred for the first time in Germany

will find that they are not immediately accepted by the birds because they do
not know them although such seeds are a necessary part of their diet. Gradually
soak them less and less until they finally eat the seed hard. You should not
forget to give them stale, white bread soaked in milk regularly. A rich variety of
greenfood is also essential when the birds eventually have good plumage,
probably after they have been with you for about a fortnight. When the Cordon
Bleus have been on their new diet for about 3 weeks, they can be moved to the
birdhouse on a warm sunny day. If it happens to be a bad summer, keep them
indoors and wait until the following summer. Birds that need to get used to the
climate should be left in their cages within the aviary. In this way, they will be
protected from adverse weather conditions and will slowly become accustomed
to other birds in the aviary. Take them indoors in their cages each night for the
first ten nights. Give them fresh drinking and bathing water, as well as food,
every day. If they appear to be healthy after three weeks, release them into the
birdhouse itself on a sunny day. Of course, fragile and sensitive birds like the
Cordon Bleus should be kept indoors during the winter.

Budgerigars
This little Australian parakeet is 20cm (7¾in) long has many admirers and can
provide great pleasure and friendship. The Budgerigar is rich in colours and

Right *Lonchura domestica* does not exist in
the wild, but is believed to be presumably
the result of crossing *Lonchura striata* and
Lonchura striata acuticauda. There are
many colour mutations. It is a good bird
for the beginner and quickly breeds in a
nesting box

Left The Sharp-tailed Munia (*Lonchura striata acuticauda*) lives in India, Indonesia and New Guinea. This ancestor of *Lonchura domestica* is as easy to keep and breed as its descendants. It mixes well with other birds in aviaries

Below left The Weavers are so called because of their beautiful nests. These are woven structures with entrance holes in the sides. This photo of a colony of weavers was taken in Africa. Normally, these birds nest in trees, but sometimes in rushes and reeds

Right The Red-billed Quelea (*Quelea quelea quelea*) comes from the region south of the Sahara, where it is now considered a nuisance because it damages agriculture and forestry. In captivity this hardy bird breeds only with great difficulty

Pages 72-3 The Peach-faced Love Bird (*Agapornis roseicollis*) originates from South-west Africa where it lives in small groups

Right A flock of wild Budgerigars looking for food and water in western Australia

A birch nesting box for parakeets. It should be hung in such a way that the birds can also roost on its roof

easy to feed and care for. It quickly becomes tame and is able to imitate many sounds including the human voice.

The enormous range of colours now available have all originated from the green of the original wild Budgerigar (*Melopsittacus undulatus*). In Australia, wild Budgerigars continue to live in the parched and inhospitable interior of the country in flocks, often of more than 1000 birds. They feed mainly on seed, a little greenfood and fruit, and also on insects during breeding time. They nest in tree holes. In captivity, they breed easily in birdhouses and quickly become very tame if sufficient attention is given to them when they are young. It makes no difference whether they are male or female because both sexes learn to repeat words and become fingertame, although it is noticeable that males learn more easily than females. Females are generally more friendly and entertaining, however, cocks are much quieter if held in the hand and do not bite quite so painfully. If you want to train budgies, you would be well advised to start while they are still young, when they have just become independent of their parents for feeding.

If you want to differentiate the sexes, look at the colour of the cere (the bits between the bill and the eye), which tends to be more violet and rounder in a young cock than in a young hen. Adult budgies can also be distinguished by their cere. The cock has a deep-blue or violet cere while that of the hen is pale brown-yellow to chocolate-brown.

If you have decided to breed budgies in order to train them, and you want to know what the sexes of the chicks will be, you should choose budgies whose breeding is sex-linked. For example, if you mate a lutino-cock (yellow) with a green hen or an Albino cock with a blue hen, you will get male offspring which are green (first pairing) or blue and all female lutinos with red eyes (first pairing) or Albinos (second pairing). With these matings, you can distinguish the sexes as soon as the chicks leave the egg, because females will always have red eyes.

You should purchase the budgies only when their cages are ready to receive them. Good pet-stores stock a variety of suitable cages with horizontal bars for the birds to climb on as well as various toys for them to play with. Seed and water containers should be fixed to the floor because in the wild the bird looks for its food on the ground. Do not put too many toys in the cage because there must be enough space for freedom of movement. They might also give all their attention to these toys, thus hindering their development in talking.

For a single bird a toy with a bell is recommended because of the fascination it

Right Fischer's Love Bird (*Agapornis fischeri*). You'll find many forms of this bird in bird markets

Below The Red-faced Love Bird (*Agapornis pullaria*)

An example of bird training

gives. Climbing is good exercise for birds' feet so the inclusion of stairs is an excellent idea – especially if the stairs are of different sizes and strengths. Tame budgies should spend time outside the cage. Don't worry too much about their excreta because it is solid and tiny, if the birds are healthy, and is easily dealt with with a piece of paper. To make the return to their cage easy, provide them with a landing point near the door of the cage. If a bird cannot return to its cage whenever it wants to, it will become nervous and therefore less easy to tame. For this reason avoid grabbing hold of the bird too often – certainly not every day. Give them a good seedmixture and periodically vary this with millet, greenfood, grit and cuttlefish bone.

If you give them a few extras like minerals and fresh tree twigs (i.e. from fruit-trees or Willows), the birds will be very healthy and often reach an age of 7, 10 or even 20 years, assuming of course that you bought healthy birds in the first place. After buying your birds, you will know for certain within the first few days whether they are healthy – particularly in the first 24 hours. When you bring your pet home, it can be moved into its cage right away. Then leave the room so that the bird can explore its new environment on its own and feed undisturbed. Renew its food and water next morning and talk to it quietly and

gently and call it by its chosen name. The name should not be too complicated and should consist of two syllables only. Not every budgie is an excellent talker but there are many which possess a surprisingly large vocabulary. Budgies which do not easily learn to talk become very tame and trusting instead and learn many amazing tricks. Tame budgies can fly freely in your livingroom. I once had a budgie which took a bath every day under a dripping water tap in the kitchen to the great delight of many visitors, a habit incidentally which many other budgies have. Tame budgies are always a great pleasure to the whole family. If you want to keep more than two of these birds, construct a birdhouse out of metal. You can also use wood but this is not quite so suitable because the birds tend to gnaw it.

Spring is breeding season. Provide sufficient nestboxes, at least as many as you have pairs. The nest box should be 18×18cm (7×7in) with a height of 25cm (10in). The flight hole of about 4cm (1½in) shold be about 5cm (2in) beneath the roof. A perch should be fixed beneath the hole so that the birds can get in and out easily. Inside the nest box put a container with a diameter of about 10cm (4in). There will be between 3 and 10 round-oval eggs although the average is

Above The Elegant Grass Parakeet (*Neophema e. elegans*) is initially rather shy

Right Male as well as female of the Red and Blue Macaw (*Ara chloroptera*) quickly learn to talk, if you start off when they are young. With good care the Macaw can reach an old age. This bird can be found in South America in the wild – with the exception of Peru and Ecuador

The Cockatiel (*Nymphicus hollandicus*) which leads a rather nomadic life. Its food consists mainly of grass seed and berries

The Rosella Parakeet (*Platycercus e. eximius*) should be kept in a cage on its own as the male is very quarrelsome. It originates from Australia as does *Nymphicus hollandicus*

Swainson's Lorikeets (*Trichoglossus haematodus moluccanus*) live in Tasmania and eastern Australia where you'll find them in Eucalyptus trees on which they feed

Below The Masked Love Bird (*Agapornis personata*). They are best kept in single pairs

four. These will hatch in about 18-20 days. The chicks have striped heads, black eyes and pink ceres. If you want to train them, you must wait until they are 5-8 weeks old when they are ready to leave the nest and feed themselves.

If you allow three broods per season you will soon have a birdhouse full of chicks which will amuse you with their capers. Before putting a pair together you should – and this goes for all pet-birds – check their condition. Catching your birds can be done with a fine-meshed net on a short handle. You can capture them either in flight or from behind, but do it calmly and do not try it more than ten times, otherwise the birds get too tired. When you have the bird, look at its nails. If they are too long, trim them with sharp nailscissors. Cuts should be made just below the vein ends, which can be clearly seen if the claws are examined against the light. Overlong claws often cause accidents because the birds get their feet caught up in the nest material when leaving the nest. Broken legs, loss of eggs or even loss of young ones can be the result. File the claws diagonally and smoothly. With climbing material such as stones, twigs and reeds in the cage, the birds' nails will tend to be worn down naturally.

Budgies do not need nesting material other than some sawdust in the nest box to protect the eggs. However, other non-parakeet birds need a lot of building

Left The Siskin (*Carduelis spinus*) is very popular with woodland bird fanciers. In Holland and Belgium it is a rare breeding bird

Below The ring round its feet tells you who bred the bird, its date of birth and other important dates

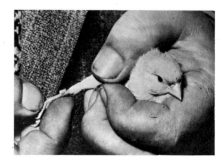

Left The Nutmeg Finch or Spice Bird (*Lonchura punctulata*) occurs in South-east Asia and in a district around Sydney, Australia since 1940

The Chaffinch (*Fringilla coelebs*) is also a
'wild song bird' with which one can breed
excellent hybrids. The finch-breeder can
distinguish various songs with these birds

The Bullfinch (*Pyrrhula pyrrhula*) is kept
in many aviaries. It breeds easily in
captivity and is able to imitate the songs of
other birds

Lazuli Bunting (*Passerina amoena*) originates from western USA and British Columbia and migrates to Mexico and to the south of the USA for the winter. During these migrations, which take place only during the night, the males fly before the females

material such as moss, coconutfibre (not too long), blades of grass, straw, small twigs, pieces of string no longer than 6cm (2in), feathers, etc.

Parakeets

The Monk Parakeet is the only member of the parrot family which builds an extensive nest and therefore needs a lot of nesting material. The Love Bird (*Agapornis*) also requires some nesting material. Twigs of Poplar and Willow would be ideal. With other parakeets, make sure that there is always moist peat or a layer of sawdust in the nest. With the exotic birds, it is advisable to pre-prepare a box with nesting material. This makes nest-building easier for them and – in the case of the Zebra Finch – avoids the risk of storage building (storage building means that a second nest is built on top of an already existing nest of eggs and, sometimes, even a third). Simply put some nesting material in the box and the birds will then build their nest. I use moist moss, which I press firmly into the bottom of the nest, having previously sprinkled some insect powder to ward off bugs and parasites. Under no circumstances should you use DDT or Lindan, which are dangerous and illegal.

For the small exotic birds, use coconut shell halves or half-open or closed nesting boxes as breeding sites. The latter type especially seems to be preferred. It should have an entrance hole with a diameter of approximately 3cm (1¼in), a base of 15×15cm (6×6in) and height of 15cm (6in). *Agapornis* breeds successfully in birchboxes with removable trays, but you could make the breeding boxes out of any wood. The minimum measurements ought to be 15×15cm (6×6in) for the base, 25cm (10in) height and an entrance hole with a diameter of 5cm (2in). The biggest of these charming miniature parrots, the Peach-faced Love-Bird (*Agapornis roseicollis*), needs a slightly bigger breeding place, i.e. 20×20cm (8×8in) base, 28cm (11in) height and entrance hole of 7cm (3in) diameter. For the even bigger parakeets, build boxes out of hard wood with measurements dependent on the size of the bird. The well-known Rose-ringed Parakeet and birds of similar size need a base of 30×30cm (12×12in), 35cm (13½in) height and an entrance hole of 8cm (3in) diameter.

If it has not built a crude nest out of twigs on the ground or in a bush the Monk Parakeet needs a box of 20×20×30cm (8×8×12in) with a hole of 8cm (3in).

The Plum-headed Parakeet will breed in a box of 18×18×28cm (7×7×11in),

Right Diamond Sparrow (*Steganopleura guttata*) originates from Australia. One can only keep a single pair in the birdhouse because they are very quarrelsome by nature

Below The Isabel Canary

Frill-canaries. This breed should always have symmetrically distributed feather curls. Its head and throat feathers should be one of two types: The Casque-type with curled feathers which gradually blend into a smooth head and the Calotte type where the frills reach a curly head

A Coloured and a Crested canary

Above left The Yorkshire Canary is the 'Gentleman of the Fancy'. It came about in 1870 in the county of Yorkshire

Above right The Gloster Fancy Canary was bred by Mrs Rogerson of Cheltenham in 1925 and made popular by the Scottish examiner J. McLey

hole 5cm (2in); the Goldchin Parakeet needs a breeding box of 25×25×35cm (10×10×13½in) hole 8cm (3in); the well-known Bourke Parakeet needs a breeding box of 18×18×28cm (7×7×11in), hole 6cm (2¼in); the Cockatiel a box of 25×25×35cm (10×10×13½in), hole 8cm (3in) (which also applies to Rosella types); the Song Parakeet likes a place of 28×28×35cm (11×11×13½in), hole 8cm (3in) diameter. All the above are inside measurements and the reader should find it easy to decide on the size of necessary breeding boxes for parakeets of about the same size as the birds named here. Below the hole should always be a little staircase. If you use deep boxes or hollowed out tree trunks of about one metre, it is important that you fix some resting places beneath the hole so that the birds can easily climb out.

If you have just bought the birds, it would be wise to ask the seller about the measurements of the nesting box which the birds used in the previous season. If the previous owner was successful with a certain type of box, it is advisable to keep to the same measurements or, if possible, to buy the box together with the birds. The roof of a breeding box should be detachable. Even better would be to have a small door in one of the side walls to be able to keep a check on things during breeding time. To avoid disturbing the birds too much, you should make checks very discreetly. An ideal time would be when the bird is taking a short flight round the birdhouse. Nests in tree hollows etc. are difficult to observe, but you will have to look now and then. Again, you should wait until the bird has left the nest and, with the help of a torch, you can then quickly check on the contents and condition of the nest. Use a mirror on a stick if it helps.

If you discover a nest with eggs which are not being incubated, do not throw the eggs away immediately, but try to accommodate them with other breeding birds. It might be that the eggs are already half-hatched. In cases where eggs have not been incubated for some time, it is not always certain that the young inside are indeed already dead. Furthermore, chicks which have fallen from the nest can often still be rescued, even if they feel cold and show no signs of life. You can often resuscitate them by warming them in your hand and by breathing upon them. After a little time you might well feel them move again and if you persevere you might be successful in reviving them. If the little bird moves, return it to its nest. The parents will start to take care of their lost chicks once they make pathetic cries for help.

Large parakeets
The big parakeets are especially colourful and elegant. They come from all parts of the tropical world and enjoy great interest in the world of birdkeeping. They

Above *Poephila cincta* originates from the East Australian interior. It is seldom seen in inhabited areas and is difficult to purchase

Right Hybrid of Canary×Goldfinch

Left The Negro Finch (*Nigrita canicapilla*)

A hybrid of *Erythrura psittacea* and
Erythrura trichroa. Because they are close
relations (both belong to the same genus)
these hybrids are easy to breed

are also popular as pets and are often kept in a roomy cage or on a stand. The
Rose-ringed Parakeet can definitely be recommended as a companion. It was
possibly the first parrot to be kept by man. The male makes a more suitable
house pet than the female. However, in a birdhouse, they should be kept as a
pair as is the case with other parakeets. The Cockatiel is also a welcome guest in
a spacious cage or birdhouse. It quickly becomes tame and may even learn to
speak a few words.

Especially attractive are various species of the genus *Aratinga* of which the
Jendya Parakeet from South America with its gold-yellow head is probably the
best known. The Tovi Parakeet originates from the same area and, with a good
diet of maize, rice, fresh buds, fruit and soaked bread, should breed without
difficulty and without interfering with its fellow-inmates. But this is not the
case with the Goldhead Parakeet. It is closely related to other South American
parakeets, but should be housed in a separate cage during breeding time.

Love Birds

Love Birds are best kept in pairs and accommodated in separate cages during
breeding time. There are different types of Love Birds which are predomin-

Above Hybrid of Nutmeg
Finch × *Lonchura domestica*

Above right Cardinal Grosbeak
(*Pyrrhuloxia sinuata*) from West Texas,
West Mexico, South New Mexico and
South-east Arizona is a rather shy bird. In
a spacious birdhouse it can be kept
together with other birds

antly green in colour with the additions of black, yellow and red feather tracts
on their heads and throats. The Masked Love Bird (*Agapornis personata*), with
its black head, red beak and white rings round the eyes, is probably the most
common of this group. If a male or female is kept on its own and is given
sufficient attention, it will learn to talk.

Lories

The keeping of lories is more difficult. They are true jewels when it comes to
colour and elegance. In the wild they feed on nectar, pollen, flower petals and a
rich assortment of fruit. Bathing is of vital necessity to these birds. They can
also become tame and are not shy of man, even in the wild. When I studied birds
in Australia, lories often accepted pieces of banana directly from my hand.
They were the lories originating from the Blue Mountains in eastern Australia.
These birds are protected in public gardens and become very popular with the
visitors. Much pleasure is to be gained from keeping these birds, whether in
cages or in birdhouses. If you clean their living quarters conscientiously, you
can keep them for years in excellent health. Pay particular attention to the floor
covering. Use absorbent paper in cages and, in birdhouses, dig the ground

Melba Finch (*Pytilia melba*) from southern and eastern Africa is an ideal cage bird. If you can obtain a pair (which is rather difficult, only few females are imported) you can quickly have breeding success. During breeding time the Melba Finch is probably a nuisance to the other birds in the aviary. The female lays 5-7 eggs, which are hatched in approximately 13 days by both parents. During this time they need an abundant supply of insects

Green Cardinal (*Gubernatrix cristata*) breeds freely in a densely planted aviary

deeply and regularly. The droppings are rather watery because of their diet of fruit, nectar and honey which is supplemented in captivity by babyfoods. Lories do not need grit or cuttlefish bone, but they like gnawing on various twigs of fruit trees, Willows or Poplars.

Ringing

As soon as the young have left their eggs you should make preparations for ringing. With most birds this is done on the 7th or 8th day. A word of caution should be introduced here regarding the ringing of canaries. After their young have been ringed, many parent birds will see the ring as something that should not be in the nest. They will therefore attempt to eject the ring even though it is attached to one of their offspring! However, it is very unlikely that they will do so once the young have reached the age when their parents no longer remove the young's excreta from the nest. You will know when this age is reached by seeing the droppings on the edge of the nest.

Matters are not helped by the rings gleaming because they are made of aluminium or copper. However, if you paint the rings black with a felt tip pen,

Above The Pectoral Sparrow (*Arremon taciturnus*) is a magnificent bird, which is even rare in its country of origin, Surinam. Its food consists of various grains. Its song is not too wonderful and it is a rather aggressive bird

The Crimson Waxbill (*Pirenestes ostrinus*) from West Africa should be accommodated in a densely-planted aviary. Its food of millet, white grain, mealworms and insects should be put out at a raised level. In general this bird is not kept in captivity

the risk is minimised even further. The rings can easily be slipped onto their
feet if you first put some Vaseline onto the toes and feet. In this way you can
'glue' the three first toes together and the back toe against the leg, then the
ringing is child's play. Afterwards wipe the feet with cotton wool.

Parakeets have zygodactyl feet, that is, two toes directed forward and two
directed backward. But the ringing can still be done in the same way with the
two front toes being 'glued' together and the back ones held against the leg. It
sometimes happens that the ring cannot be pushed far enough to free the back
toes. However, this can be overcome without risk by freeing the toes with a
matchstick. Ringing is best done towards the evening because by then parents
have finished the daily cleaning. Next morning check whether all rings are still
in place, because lively young can lose them. If you do not notice this until later,
you have the problem of ringing adult birds which is impossible with closed
rings. Ringing is necessary if you intend to exhibit your birds because the rings
give details of all the important dates concerning those birds.

Woodland birds

If you want to keep woodland birds you should have a birdhouse with plenty of
dense vegetation, hiding places and weed seeds. The birdhouse should have as

Above The Java Sparrow or Rice Finch (*Padda oryzivora*) occurs in South-east Asia and East Africa where it was introduced by man. Previously it existed only on Java and Bali. It can easily be kept in a cage or outdoor aviary and breeds freely

Right The Red-whiskered Bulbul (*Pycnonotus jocosus*) originates from India and is a friendly bird which sings beautifully. It loves a quiet densely-grown aviary

natural an environment as possible. Sex differentiation is a problem with the goldfinch, because male and female can hardly be distinguished. But if you take the bird in your hand and blow at its chest and stomach feathers, you can tell the sex: the male has yellow feathers whereas the female has only brown feathers in her plumage.

Experimental breeding

Breeding for colour is also possible with woodland birds. Furthermore, cross-breeding between quite different birds, such as a goldfinch with a canary, can sometimes be achieved. Such cross-breeding will result in what are known as wild colour females and split males. These combinations are possible because of the sex-linked nature of colours.

Pairing split males with wild colour females will produce wild colour and split males as well as wild colour and colour deviating females. A crossing of split males with colour deviating females results in colour deviating and split males as well as colour deviating and normal females. If you pair deviating colour with deviating colour then you will get deviating colour in both sexes. This is a

Above The Fairy Bluebird (*Irena puella*) from India, Moluccas and Indochina. Close examination of its skeletal frame indicates that it belongs to the Piroles or Drongos rather than to the Bulbuls

Right The Long-tailed Finch (*Poephila acuticauda*) lives in North-west Australia.

sex-linked variety as already referred to in breeding budgerigars. It works in the following way.

Every bird is in possession of a pair of sex-determining chromosomes (carriers of the hereditary characteristics). The male has two X chromosomes whereas the female has one X and one Y chromosome (as in the case of butterflies). It is the reverse with all other animals including humans. When the male X chromosome and the female X chromosome merge, the result is male offspring (XX). However, if the X chromosome of the male merges with the Y chromosome of the female, the result is female offspring (XY).

In effect, the Y of the female means that it does not possess a second X chromosome and it follows that it can give its hereditary characteristics to its sons, but not to its daughters. Hence a pairing of wild colour with deviating colour produces only wild colour male offspring, which are split for deviating colour. Females can never be split. Split means hidden, that is, males can pass on deviating colour to their progeny although they show no outward signs of having that colour element themselves. For example, a split male with a wild colour female produces wild colour and split males as well as wild colour and colour deviating females. You can see therefore that a female can never be split. The X chromosome is decisive in determining sex.

It is generally through pure coincidence if you find several hybrids in a nest of young. If you consciously want to breed them, you will find success hard to achieve. It is a shame that most hybrids are infertile, but the Red Canary was produced from cross-breeding Canary with Scarlet South American Crest Siskin (*Carduelis cucuillata*). A hybrid Siskin or goldfinch is an ornament in any aviary.

But you should not attempt to pair just any birds because they appear to be compatible in size and species. Although they might produce offspring quickly and frequently, you will probably be disappointed with the end results. I am thinking of the pairing, for example, of *Agapornis roseicollis* with *Agapornis fischeri* or Splendid with Turquoise Parakeet. These are such closely related bird species, that you cannot really refer to them as hybrids. Perhaps a better name would be the French expression 'Metise'. These Metises are even fertile. In both of the above examples you will get offspring which are neither one thing nor the other. In addition, you will find later on that a pairing of these can result in the degeneration of form and especially colour and markings. Furthermore, Metises are also often crossed back with their parents (inbreeding) with a resultant motley collection of offspring which will not achieve great results in

Above Diamond Dove (*Geopelia cuneata*) from Australia. Never keep more than one pair in an aviary.

Left Victoria Crowned Pigeon (*Goura victoria*) is a precious bird, which can be found from Yellow Finch Bay to Astrolabe Bay, New Guinea

Right Green Singing Finch (*Serinus mozambicus*) from Tropical Africa is an excellent songster who likes plenty of room

exhibition. But the greatest danger is that the purity of that species might be lost. I have consciously named Love Birds because, at the moment, you can find many Metises of the Fischer's Love Bird in birdmarkets, all of which are 'impure' birds. It is therefore unfortunate that it can take countless pairings to get back to breeding pure Love Birds.

Within the last few years, hybrids have appeared from the cross-breeding of the normal Yellow Canary with the Border. The progeny are neither like father nor mother, but somewhere in between and therefore of little value to a bird-fancier. Such crossings do not result in desirable hybrids. It is different of course if through back-crossing you improve form and/or colour, which was the case with the above mentioned Siskin and Canary. This was done by introducing the red factor into the plumage and finally resulted in a Red Canary.

In the previous chapter we mentioned *Lonchura domestica*. This too is a hybrid and is more popular than the yellow Border hybrid. Most hybrids are the descendants of carefully selected birds. For example, a Canary with a bird renowned for its song.

They should be kept in pairs in breeding cages or, if possible, in an aviary,

Golden-breasted Avadavat (*Amandava subflava*) comes from south of the Sahara in Africa. It will breed in an aviary but not always successfully. Many nests are built, but not all of them raise young

where more natural circumstances encourage quick pairing and successful breeding. For success you should separate the pair in question and let them be together again seven months before the breeding season so that they can get acquainted and hopefully become attached to each other. If it is at all possible select young birds which have never paired before.

The Cape Canary (*Serinus canicollis*), for example, can be crossed with a Gold Agath, Green-singing Finch or dominant White Canary; the European Siskin with Lemon Agath, the Black-headed Siskin with Gold or Green Agath; the Green Finch with Norwich; the Mexican Karmin Bullfinch with Yorkshire; the European Canary with Gloster Corona. You can also get lovely hybrids from Greenfinch with Water Finch, Green Singing Finch with Goldfinch, Goldfinch with Bullfinch and Greenfinch with Bullfinch. The most beautiful hybrids of all result from Red-tail Canary with Goldfinch which, incidentally, are very expensive and rare.

Tropical birds can also be paired with each other. Lately the hybrid *Lonchura domestica* with Zebra-Finch has become very popular as well as *Lonchura domestica* with African Silverbill (or the reverse), Reed Finch and Nutmeg Finch. In addition, the hybrids of the various species of Australian Grass Finch are in great demand. There are many possibilities as long as it is done sensibly. But some birds are not suitable for hybridization. An example is provided by the Australian parrots of the genus *Platycercus*.

They are so closely related that hybrids from the different species have little to recommend themselves. A further reason is that there is an export embargo from Australia and if pure birds are to be bred from existing stock outside that country, then they should be kept genetically pure for as long as possible.

6 Colouring and song

The canary

For brilliance of colour and liveliness of song, the canary has few equals and it has been a widely popular pet for more than four centuries. The canary makes few demands on its keeper. It is easy to care for, highly adaptable and extremely companionable. As a caged bird, the canary requires only simple lodgings which need not take up much room in the home. Given regular attention, it will become extremely tame and fly onto your shoulder, head or finger. If it is a cock bird, it will also sing in its cage to its heart's content.

Canaries are usually divided into two groups; the Continental-Type Breeds and the English-Type Breeds. Belonging to the first group are the Parisian Frill, Padovan Frill, the North Dutch Frill and the South Dutch Frill, the Swiss Frill, the Italian Humpback Frill (*Gibber Italicus*), the Belgian Humpback, the Munich, the Berner and the Crest Canary.

The English-Type Breeds are the Scotch Fancy, the Border, the Fife Fancy, the Norwich, the Yorkshire, the two types of Gloster canaries (Consort and Corona), the Crested, the Lancashire and the Lizard. Basically, the breeding of these birds does not differ from that of song or colour canaries. Firstly, it is

A wild Canary (*Serinus canaria*) ancestor of all canaries

Above Three Red Canaries. This variety owes its origin to cross-breeding the Hooded Siskin and the Canary

Right The Blue Canary is really green with dominant white and blue factor. The blue is a so-called structure colour. When breeding time begins the cloaca is turned outwards and directed slightly to the front. We can see this if we blow the feathers beneath the tail

important that you make a critical selection and observe the essentials laid down in the official standard charts.

The difference in song of male and female can be noticed quite distinctively, especially just before breeding season. Breeding can be done by pair-breeding or change-breeding (one cock with various hens). Ensure that breeding takes place in a warm environment, ideally indoors, with temperatures of about 20°C (68°F). The easiest types to breed are Lizards, Glosters and Crested canaries. Other types can sometimes cause difficulties. If you wish to breed Lizards, check that the parents-to-be have good oval caps. These caps should not be fully developed in both parents because their offspring's caps will be far too big and too full. The most successful pairing is achieved by putting a bird with a full cap and intensive colour with one which has a broken cap and has greyish colour. It might be of interest to know that Lizards can only be exhibited in the first year, because after their first moult they will have 'bleached' quills and thus would not achieve many points. But for breeding they are suitable because their descendants will be pure Lizards. Lizards are very free breeders, often acting as foster parents for young form and posture canaries which are often neglected by their parents. The Gloster is also very prolific and makes a good fosterparent. The only right pairing here is Corona (crest) with Consort (smooth head).

Left Coloured canaries are very popular nowadays. There are canaries with or without red pigmentation. The latter include the Green, Blue and Brown Canaries

Below left A female Gold-yellow Canary. A rarely used name for this bird is 'Dark-yellow canary'. The Light-yellow canary is often described as 'Straw-yellow'.

Below The hen, when ready for breeding, has a cloaca which does not lie in the direction of the tail but is turned upwards

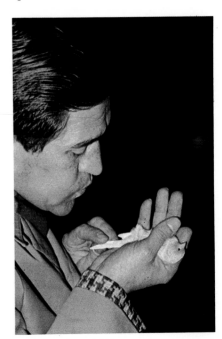

Many useful nesting opportunities have been invented. Strict guidelines for ideal breeding places are difficult to lay down. It is often a matter of experiment, although most species have their own individual preferences

Right A canary nest with eggs

Below A Budgerigar cage with entrance hole on the right-hand side so that the ingoing bird does not damage its eggs or young ones. The nest is almost always at the left-hand side of the box.

The Grey Singing Finch (*Serinus leucopygius*) breeding in a canary nest. It originates from North Africa and can be dangerous to smaller birds during breeding time

Below The nest of the Parrot-finch *Erythrura psittacea* in a flower pot. The bird occurs in the wild in New Caledonia. During breeding time the temperature should ideally be 25°C 80°F.

Above The nest of *Lonchura domestica* in an open nest box

Right A nest of young *Serinus leucopygius*

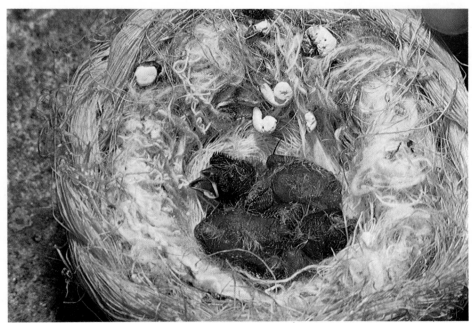

If you want to breed canaries, care must be taken in selection in order to achieve the best possible results. When breeding time arrives, the cloaca protrudes and you can see the bulge if you blow the feathers beneath the tail. The female, when ready for breeding, has a cloaca which does not run in the direction of the tail. The first consideration is to separate males from females right from the start. This is best done in February. Ideally, you should provide the birds with spacious breeding cages. Allocate three or four females to their own breeding cage where they will do their nest building. The female, which completes her nest first, receives the male and mating takes place soon afterwards. When the first egg is laid, the male will go to female number two and so on.

However, placing a pair together for the duration of the breeding process is also possible, but the cock often becomes restless when the fledglings appear and starts to bother the female again by continuously wishing to mate.

The hen then becomes confused and may start to build a new nest. After she lays new eggs, the young from the first clutch become neglected by her. Of course, such a situation should be avoided by the early separation of male from female, as the latter can well rear the young by herself.

A brooding Cape Canary (*Serinus canicollis*)

Breeding time starts around mid March. The hen can be heard to call for the cock and this is the sign that she is ready for breeding. Provide a small nesting basket in the breeding cage together with some nesting material and you will find that the hen starts to build a nest almost immediately. You should only allow the mate into the same cage when the hen has completed the nest. He will make breeding readiness known by singing vigorously. Take care that you do not introduce a male to a hen which is not ready for breeding because this will incur difficulties which can lead to bloody fights. It goes without saying that the breeding cages should be left in peace. Do not make the mistake of watching the breeding process every day, because this will result in their abandoning the nest. Leave the birds to themselves.

The first egg can normally be expected around 7 o'clock in the morning. At noon, carefully remove the egg with a plastic spoon from the nest and replace it with a dummy which you can buy in any pet-shop. Put the real egg in a box with dry sand together with a note giving details of the date and the number of the relevant hen. You can expect the second egg on the following day when you repeat the above process. Continue the procedure until you have four eggs. The reason for this is to ensure that the eggs all hatch at the same time. Turn the real

Young Parrot-finch (*Erythrura psittacea*). Because these birds nest in rather dark hollows, the chicks have reflecting organs which mark their beaks

Left The familiar Greenfinch (*Chloris chloris*) in its nest with young ones

eggs in the sand-pit once a day. When the hen has laid all four eggs, remove the dummies (the best time is in the evening) and return the real eggs. The eggs usually hatch out thirteen days later. It is recommended to check on the sixth or seventh day whether the eggs are fertile. Fertile eggs appear dark and brightly coloured, whereas infertile eggs tend to be transparent. You can 'X-ray' the eggs with the aid of a shoe-box. In the lid cut a hole which is slightly smaller than the egg. Put a torch in the box and then 'X-ray' the eggs in a dark room. Fertile eggs, unlike infertile ones, hardly let light penetrate.

After you have inspected all the eggs, let the hen incubate them again. Further checks are now unnecessary. During incubation, gradually increase the egg-food. Once the chicks have hatched, the parents will feed this to their young. On the fourth day, gradually start to give them green food as well. Together with the rearing food you can also offer soaked seed.

At the beginning, the parent birds clear the nest of the excreta which is 'wrapped' in thin skins. After each feed they wait until the chick puts its bottom up in the air and they pick away the excreta before it can dirty the nest. This lasts for one week. This is also a good time to ring the chicks. At the age of 16 to 17 days the chicks will have completed plumage and will leave the nest. It will not take long before they are feeding themselves. Of course, the normal seed is still too hard for their weak bills and you should grind the seed to begin with. You can do this with a rolling-pin. When the chicks are 22 days old, they are almost fully-grown. They should then be removed from their parents and housed in a spacious cage where they can develop well. It is a good idea to put the young birds in with an old hen which might feed them now and again. Alternatively, you could put the mother-hen in with her youngsters for a few days. This is probably a better idea because not only will the young accept food from her more easily, but also because she will tend to move around more, thus speeding up her recovery. After a few days, the hen can be returned to her breeding cage to rear a second brood. When they have spent about one week in their own cage, the chicks will be able to eat normal seed without difficulty and can be regarded as being independent. In the period leading up to their first moulting, accommodate the birds in a bigger cage. During the first moulting, make sure that the birds have plenty of bathing opportunities and a good choice of seed and other food supplies. Furthermore, take care that the cage is completely draughtproof.

Canaries are not normally considered fully independent until they have completed their first moulting successfully. All fluff should vanish from their heads and plumage. Keep a close eye on young canaries because they sometimes tend to pluck each others feathers or their own. The habit can become so bad that they inflict injuries and actually bleed. The cause of this behaviour can often be overcrowding in the cage or boredom. The problem needs to be recognised and dealt with promptly. If you try to ignore it, you might end up with not only victims but also with birds which continue the bad habit for many years. If it is caused by boredom, hang up flax threads and strung-up weed seeds (Nettle, Birch, Alder, Thistle) to provide them with alternative pecking material.

The breeding season finishes towards the end of June. If all went well, the pairs will have reared three or four broods and may now enjoy a well-earned rest in a spacious habitat.

Parrots

Parrots are colourful birds which enjoy great popularity at present. With good care, they have life expectancies of many decades. There are some parrots which have been in one family from one generation to the next.

Although its plumage is not as colourful as other parrots, the African Grey is one of the most popular of its kind because of its ability to mimic human voices and other sounds. A tame African Grey Parrot, male or female, will only display

its abilities if it is allowed to move around the house each day and if its owner plays with it.

Much more colourful are the many kinds of Amazon Parrots. Some of them are extremely noisy whereas others have very friendly characters and quickly become tame. If taught early, they can learn to speak surprisingly well.

The food for these parrots should consist of a seed mixture which includes sunflower seed, some hemp, maize and oats. They are also fond of fruit, nuts and greenfood. Some enjoy carrots, turnips, celery and even artichokes. Make sure that they are not given cake, sweets, lumps of sugar or food remnants because they will become too fat or suffer intestinal disorders. It is absolutely necessary that parrots are given grit and clean water daily. Cuttlefish bone, mineral blocks and soft wood should always be available for them to keep their beaks in trim.

Most parrots can be accommodated in the common-place round or rectangular cages. But make sure that the cage is of solid constuction because parrots have surprisingly strong bills. To keep their plumage brilliant, parrots should be sprayed regularly with clean water.

Macaws

Much larger birds are the magnificent Macaws with their brilliant blue, yellow, green and red colours and their huge beaks which they use to crack nuts open in the wild.

Their appearance belies their character because they behave very tenderly and gently towards their keepers. In captivity they will eat peanuts, sunflowerseed, maize, canary seed, oats, etc. Fruit like apples, pears, cherries (without stones) and berries are welcome to them and ought to be supplied at least twice a week.

Of course, this giant cannot be caged but should be chained to a stand of light metal or hardwood (chain minimum 20cm (8in), but maximum 30cm (12in)) where it will be able to move about and beat its wings without damaging its long tail. A tame Macaw can also be allowed to wander about the garden freely.

Their plumage requires special attention. It should be sprayed regularly or they should be given plenty of opportunity to bathe or shower. Macaws love to stand under a shower of rain on a warm summer's day. They also learn to speak well but you have to get used to their voice-tones which sound hard and croaky.

Cockatoos

Cockatoos are very attractive birds which, despite their noisiness, are most charming and become very attached to their owners. They are mainly white

Right Guarouba Parakeet (*Aratinga guarouba*) from South America

Left The African Grey Parrot (*Psittacus erithacus*) occurs in West and Central Africa and is popular because of his great talent for imitation

The Military Macaw (*Ara militaris*) lives in small groups of 4-30 birds in tropical South America

Right Multicoloured Parakeet (*Psephotus varius*)

with yellow or pink markings and often carry beautiful big crests which they can erect like a fan when excited or seeking attention.

Some cockatoos learn to talk and become very tame. They can be kept in spacious parrot cages but also on T-stands which they seem to prefer, in general. If you do keep a cockatoo in a cage, you must give it opportunity to walk about freely and regularly. Otherwise the bird might develop gout. The best known is probably the Lesser Sulphur-Crested Cockatoo from Australia. The Inca Cockatoo from Central Australia (about 40cm (15½in)) is also common and might even breed in spacious aviaries. The Sulphur-Crested Cockatoo has also been known to breed in captivity.

Cockatoos require a good choice of food among which should be sunflower seeds, hemp, maize, rye, apples, berries, nuts and various greenfood. They are also fond of peas which they shell themselves.

Mynahs
We have referred to the canary with its colourful plumage and beautiful song and we have mentioned parrots and cockatoos with their abilities to mimic human voices. The next bird to be considered also has the ability to mimic

113

Hyazint-Ara (*Anodorhynchus hyacinthus*) is the biggest of the Aras. An adult often has a length of one metre (3ft).

Right Blue-yellow Ara (*Ara ararauna*) learns to speak well. It occurs in South America. Like most other Aras, it is a forest inhabitant. The beak is suited to this environment because it is used as a third foot when climbing trees

sound and is much more successful at doing so than parrots or cockatoos. We refer, of course, to the Mynah. In many countries Mynahs are the most popular of cage and aviary birds. They come from India and the Far East and belong to the starling family. Ornithologists differentiate eleven different kinds which all live in groups. Only during the breeding season do pairs keep to themselves. Mynahs can be found in jungles and bamboo-forests, but by no means are they shy of inhabited places. Often they can be found in parks and gardens of bigger towns. In their countries of origin they are taken out of the nest when very young and hand-reared with love and devotion until they are adult. In this way they become extremely tame and quickly learn to talk. They can imitate the human voice so well that it can easily be mistaken for that of their keeper, because they even manage to hit the right pitch perfectly. I have known birds that were kept in factories which could imitate the noise of the machines to perfection. I came across one Mynah in America, which was kept in an office and could imitate the sound of a typewriter – very useful when the staff felt lazy!

The food of these fascinating birds consists largely of a mixture of fresh and dried insects, bread-crumbs, dried fruit (cut-up) and fresh soft fruit. Pet-shops

Above The Sulphur-crested Cockatoo (*Cacatua galerita*) with erect crest. If a cockatoo is threatened or wants to impress the opposite sex, it erects its crest

Left The Red-blue Ara (*Ara macao*) is also known as the Red- or Yellow-wing Ara, Maycao or Ara kanga. It originates from Central and South America and is very popular in zoos. It can reach an age of more than 20 years

Above Red-tailed Black Cockatoo
(*Calyptorhynchus banksi*) from Australia

Right A threatening Blue-yellow Ara
(Ara ararauna)

nowadays sell a good mixture for Mynahs, which you can supplement with soaked sultanas and raisins. Live insects, raw mincemeat (lean), raw meat cut into cubes and hard boiled eggs are welcome and should be included in its weekly diet. Grapefruit and oranges are also much appreciated by them. Grated carrots can be given together with the oranges. It is important to know which food the young Mynah was given before you acquired it so that the same diet can be continued initially in order to avoid stomach disorders. This should be done with any newly bought bird. Many birds have died because they were given the standard food that was thought right for them, but without consideration of their previous diets.

Mynahs should be kept in roomy cages constructed in such a way that they can be easily and quickly cleaned. It is therefore advisable to have a metal cage with front bars and closed walls. Bigger Mynahs can also be kept in parrot cages. Extreme hygiene is necessary. Put down a good floor covering (not newspaper) in the cage each day and sprinkle sand on it. I personally use wrapping paper with the matt side up. This paper absorbs well and needs to since their excreta is rather wet and messy.

If the mynah is kept in an open cage, it will enjoy a rainshower in summer time. But you will need to clean and dry the cage thoroughly afterwards.

117

You begin the training of Mynahs in the same way as Budgerigars and parrots. As soon as the Mynah feels at home and has become used to its keeper, cage and food, it will start to imitate sounds. This is the time to teach a few simple words with each one being mastered before going on to the next. It is also important that there is always only one person doing the training. Otherwise the bird becomes confused if it is offered too many different sounds. The keeper should also take care that the bird has sufficient exercise. Once it is really tame, it can sometimes fly freely around the garden. Before you risk this, the bird should be finger-tame and obey when called by its name. Plenty of movement exercise is essential for the Mynah. Lack of exercise will result in the bird becoming lazy and fat with the keeper losing interest.

Above The Hill Mynah (*Gracula religiosa*)

Right The little Cuban Finch (*Tiaris canora*) is a popular and easy to breed bird. It loves honey combs

Left An intensive Red Canary

Below The Java Beo (*Eulabes intermedia javana*). They are excellent imitators and speakers

7 Keeping your bird in good health

It is impossible to deal in a book such as this with all the ailments which can afflict birds in cages and aviaries. However, this chapter will attempt to deal with the more important ones.

A sick bird is usually easy to identify: its plumage will be fluffed up, it will look listless and dull, be very inactive and will not feed well. If you are not sure whether your bird is sick or not, especially rarer species, you should consult a veterinary surgeon.

An infected bird should be put in a 'hospital' cage which is equipped with heating lamps and a thermometer, ensuring that the temperature gradually increases to 30°C (86°F). If an infectious illness has been diagnosed, the cage or aviary will have to be disinfected. This can be done by removing or deeply digging over the sand and cleaning the perches and any plants. It would be even better to entirely renew all of these.

After handling a sick bird, make sure that you wash your hands well before turning to the next patient. A good book on bird ailments is useful or refer to a vet if any cause for concern arises.

Left Superb Tanager (*Tangara fastuosa*)

Right A pair of Melba Finches (*Pytilia melba*). Neither the Tanager nor the Melba Finch possess a very dense plumage

121

Zebra Finches (*Taeniopygia guttata*) are as common in Australia as sparrows are here. Often one can encounter flocks of hundreds near waterplaces. They move from one place to another in search of food and stay in contact with each other by callnotes. Today there is an embargo on the export of these birds from Australia, but the number of Zebra Finches outside Australia is vast

Below Two male specimens

Above A sick Budgerigar with limp wings and swollen eyes. Healthy birds sleep mostly on one leg

Above right The Fruit or Blue-yellow Tanager must, like all other Tanagers (*Thraupidae*) be accommodated in a spacious aviary

Right Green Avadavat (*Amandava formosa*) from India is a quiet bird which stays mainly on the ground. At breeding time it builds a big globular nest

Below Red Avadavat or Strawberry Finch (*Amandava amandava*) from India, Sumatra, Java and Borneo. It is a small, hardy bird which breeds easily in a densely planted aviary

Tuberculosis

Tuberculosis is caused by bacteria (*Mycobacterium avium*) and infection takes place via the droppings of an infected bird. It can also be caused by bacteria on eggshells or human beings suffering from tuberculosis. To avoid the risk of tuberculosis, the highest level of hygiene is very important. In addition, make sure your birds have plenty of fresh air (without draughts, of course) and lots of sunshine. A bird which suffers from tuberculosis loses weight, does not feed and will show blood in its droppings. If an infection is suspected, separate all of your birds from each other immediately. Don't lose any time in disinfecting your cage or aviary with Cresol, 3% Formalinsolvent or Chloramin. Any affected bird will eventually die from the infection because, sadly, there is no known cure for tuberculosis in birds.

Make sure your healthy birds are given plenty of vitamins and minerals. Keep them separated for a few weeks until it is clear that the infection has been contained. Often tuberculosis appears as swollen limbs. Many an infected bird will die as a result of a tear in the liver.

Dead birds should be burned and not, as is often the case, stuffed because the danger of contamination remains.

Above Indian Nonpareil (*Erythrura prasina*) from India, Java, Sumatra, Borneo, takes about 1½ years to regain its bright colours in an aviary. This process can be speeded up by feeding it insects

Left Orange-cheeked Waxbill (*Estrilda melpoda*) preening itself. Once acclimatised, it can be put in a sheltered outdoor aviary

Paratyphus

Paratyphus, a disease of the intestines, the symptoms of which appear in various forms. The most common form is caused by *Salmonella typhimurinum* bacteria, which are also dangerous to all other mammals including humans. The illness subsides quickly with young birds but very slowly with adult birds. Paratyphus is often carried by raw eggshells which are fed to birds and is often the result of poor hygiene. However, more often than not, mice and other rodents are the chief culprits for carrying and spreading bacteria. Therefore, you must make sure that rodents are never able to get into or even near birdhouses.

Infected birds have no appetite, shiver with cold and sleep a lot. The droppings look white-yellow or green as is the case with diarrhoea and the vent (back passage) is very dirty. Often the birds can hardly keep their balance and their eyes discharge a slimy liquid. (It should be noted that these are symptoms of acute cases of the disease.) The birds become inactive and lose weight. If their condition improves you should still keep them isolated. They need to be checked by a qualified veterinary surgeon who will give them antibiotics.

Above A Tiger Finch, dyed with ink: a method which unscrupulous bird dealers use to sell birds under fantastic sounding names. When the bird moults, the buyer realizes he has been swindled

Left The Pekin Robin (*Leiothrix lutea*) should not be accommodated together with smaller birds because it plunders nests occasionally

Right The Orange-bellied Leafbird (*Chloropsis hardwickei*) from India feeds on fruit

Below The Green Honeycreeper (*Chlorophanes spiza*) belongs to the *Emberizidae* family

Psittacosis and Ornithosis

Also known as 'parrot illness', this can be transmitted to humans (pneumonia). Parrots can suffer from the former which is an illness caused by the virus *Muyagawanella psittaci*. Other species of birds can suffer from Ornithosis which is caused by the virus *ornithosis*. Parrots normally import this illness from their life in the wild which is why parrot imports are strictly controlled, with birds kept in quarantine for some time. Affected birds do not want to feed, fluff up their feathers and their excreta is grey-green. If the course of the disease enters its final stage, nervous disorders can be found in those affected. For example, birds can no longer sit on their perches. With antibiotics, it is possible in the early stages to kill the virus and save the birds. But chances of recovery are usually slim with the affected birds dying quickly. Remember that dead birds must be burned.

Respiratory ailments

Ailments of the respiratory system are very common. Sudden temperature changes can cause chills and bronchitis. The birds' nostrils become blocked with the result that they suffer from difficult and laboured breathing. Catarrh is

Above Yellow-legged Honeycreeper (*Cyanerpes caeruleus chocoana*) from the South American forests, where it feeds on nectar and fruit, mostly over-ripe oranges

Above left The Hooded Pitta (*Pitta sordida*) lives in India, South-east Asia, Korea and Japan. It lives in trees and bushes where it searches for insects and spiders

Below Golden-breasted Avadavat (*Amandava subflava*) is a very small bird from Africa which needs to be kept in a heated room during winter

accompanied by wheezing and rasping. You must isolate a sick bird and accommodate it in a clinically prepared cage where the temperature should gradually rise to 40°C (102°F). Wash its bill with lukewarm water and dissolve antibioticum in the drinking water. Use a dark infra-red lamp for heating.

Digestive disorders

These can be caused by draught, cold, cold baths or contaminated drinking water or food. The extreta is slimy and of grey/grey-brown colour. The area around the cloaca is swollen and red and the feathers are dirty. Do not give the affected bird any green or soft food but feed *Papaver somniferum, Setaria italica* and administer antibiotic drugs. Keep the cloaca and area around it clean. If constipation occurs then feed green food and trickle some olive oil into its bill. Glauber salt can be dissolved in the bird's drinking water at a ratio of 1:200.

Illnesses which result usually from nutrition disorders include gout and arthritis. Poisoning by uric acid often means damage to the kidneys with excess salt being deposited onto the peritoneum, heartchamber and into the wing and feet joints. Administer vitamin A to larger birds like parrots. Much smaller birds can be given ¼ tablet Atophan up to 0.5 g.

Moulting and feather disorders

To ensure a quick and successful moult, observe absolute hygiene in the bird's accommodation and make sure that it has a humid atmosphere and as much sun as possible. The addition of insects to the bird's diet is recommended. It is essential that birds be kept as quiet as possible during moulting. If they fly awkwardly against the bars during this time, their new feathers might break resulting in heavy bleeding. If this happens, administer Murmil (Bayer) which contains vitamin H. Birds can also have the unpleasant habit of plucking their own or other birds' feathers. It even happens that parents pluck their own chicks bald. When this occurs, it often means that their diet is inadequate. Boredom can also be the cause – especially with the larger birds. Immediate action is called for if the bird is to be cured of this vice. It should be put in a special cage containing lots of fresh wood to chew, bacon-rind and sisal-string. In addition, you should provide a great deal of the right food plus vitamin preparations and mineral supplements. However, the cure often takes a very long time.

Loss of feathers can also be caused by mites. Microtox powder (Bayer) can be of help here. The cage or aviary, particularly perches and nesting boxes, should be thoroughly cleaned and disinfected.

Eye infections

These are often found in newly imported birds and are usually caused by inadequate standards of hygiene during transportation. However, dust or poor feeding can also be the causes. Such infections can be quickly overcome by using antibiotics and supplementary vitamins.

Mineral deficiency

Lack of essential minerals, especially calcium, can result in rickets – particularly in young birds. Those affected will have soft, bent legs on which they can hardly stand. Make sure that they have sufficient intake of vitamins B and D.

Parasites

Parasites can be divided into those which are present on birds (ectoparasites) and those present in birds (endoparasites). Endoparasites can be found in the intestines, in the blood and in the body tissue. The parasite known as coccidia causes infections in the intestines resulting in slimy and bloody excreta. Your veterinary surgeon can prescribe sulfonamides which will treat though not prevent this condition. The excreta can infect other animals, therefore utmost hygiene is called for.

Left Male Banded Pitta (*Pitta guajana*)

Right The Golden Tanager (*Tangara arthus goodsoni*) from South America is still a rare sight in aviaries. A pair of Golden Tanagers cannot be housed with other birds. At breeding time they persecute any 'intruder'

Mites (Ectoparasites) cause 'chalk legs'. They bore holes, which look like scabs, in the skin of the feet. Apply olive oil or Vaseline to the infected places in order to seal off the oxygen supply to the mites. This treatment will kill off the parasites, but it can take some time before it is effective. Prevention is always better than cure, so keep any infected birds away from others to avoid the spread of the infection.

Worms can also live in the intestines (threadworm, maw-worm, hair-worm). Threadworms are mostly found in newly imported birds. Maw-worms appear in cage and aviary birds which have been bred by humans for generations. Healthy birds become infected by the excreta of infected birds. With most species of birds administer oral Mintic (ICI) but, with rare species, use Promintic (ICI) after consultation with your veterinary surgeon.

Bacteria

The most common form of bacteria causing illnesses in birds is *Escherichia 'coli'*. If anything is wrong with the bird's food, the bacteria, which live in the intestines, multiply rapidly, often resulting in the death of the bird. Sulfonamides are known to be a good cure and can be obtained from your veterinary surgeon.

Egg-binding

Egg-binding is the inability of the hen to pass a fully developed egg. This can be caused by many different factors including sudden cold weather conditions or too little minerals or vitamins. The affected bird, often a young hen, will be found huddled on the floor of the cage with ruffled-up feathers and can hardly stand on its legs. Wrap the hen in a soft, moist cloth and hold her over a container of warm, slightly steaming water. In more severe cases, apply a few drops of olive oil into the cloaca. Take great care that the egg does not break inside the hen because the sharp shell can cause fatal injuries.

When the breeding season starts, ensure a warm temperature for the hen and mix a few drops of cod-liver oil in its feed and make plenty of minerals available.

On very rare occasions, hens have difficulty passing what are known as 'wind eggs'. The difference between these and proper eggs can be felt with the fingers. The former are soft and give way whereas the latter feels hard. If a wind egg is diagnosed, squash it with your fingers and then keep the bird isolated with treatment from an infra-red lamp.

Appendix

Seed mixtures

For canaries and woodland birds

Canary seed (*Phalaris canariensis*)	45%
Rape seed (*Brassica rapa*)	35%
Cabbage seed	8%
Niger seed (*Guizotia abyssinica*)	2%
Broken oats (*Avena sativa*)	2%
Hemp (*Cannabis sativa*)	2%
Poppy seed (*Papaver somniferum*)	1%
White lettuce seed	2%
Linseed (*Linum usitatissimum*)	2%
Plantain seed	1%

For small exotic birds

		For big tropical birds	
Senegal barley	70%		
Canary seed	10%	Millet	75%
Red millet	10%	White seed	15%
Niger seed	5%	Red millet	7%
Japanese millet	5%	Niger seed	3%

For Budgerigars and Love Birds

Millet	75%
Shelled oats	5%
Hemp	5%
Niger seed	5%

For the big English show species, alter the proportions to 45% for White seed and 40% for Millet.
For big show parakeets, add white sunflower kernel (*Helianthus annuus*) 10-15% to the above mentioned mixture.

For parrots and similar birds

Sunflower kernel	45%
White seed	30%
Millet	15%
Unshelled oats	5%
Hemp	5%

Types of seeds

1 Poppyseed (*Papaver somniferum*): 21% albumen and 50% fat.

2 Millet (*Setaria italica*): collective name. Millet is found in the ears of corn and has ± 14% albumen and 5% fat, vitamin B and is rich in iron, potassium, manganese and copper.

3 Oats (*Avena sativa*): rich in argon, fibrous material, calcium, vitamin B and E, albumen (12%) and fats (± 5%). Provide oats shelled or broken.

4 Hemp (*Cannabis sativa*): rich in argon, vitamin E, +20% albumen and 30% fat, oily.

5 Linseed (*Linum usitatissimum*): 23% albumen, 35% fat. Rich in Amino-acids, argon and vitamin E, oily.

6 Millet (*Panicum miliaceum*): in yellow, red and white, latter is soft. 12% albumen, 4% fat, rich in Methoinin and leucin.

7 Niger seed (*Guizotia abyssinica*): ± 20% albumen, 40% fat, rich in vitamin E.

8 Rape seed (*Brassica rapa*): 20% albumen, 44% fat. The use of sulphuric seed (sweeter) is strongly advised against.

9 White seed (canary seed) (*Phalaris canariensis*): 14% albumen, 4.5% raw fats. The Moroccan white seed is to be given preference.

10 Sunflowerkernel (*Helianthus annuus*): available in white, striped and black. Rich in albumen (± 15%), minerals and vitamin E.

Other nourishment

Insectfood should be given daily in earthen-ware, china or glass vessels. Always take away old food remnants. A good mixture is: breadcrumbs, dried meat and/or fishmeal, dried insects (flies, spiders, ant chrysalis, etc.) and fresh ant chrysalis. Stir with milk or water until it becomes crumbly. The mixture may not be wet and sticky.

Universalfood is for insect-eating birds, like the Pekin Robin, Beo, starlings, etc. It is insectfood, enriched with minerals, honey, and extra ant chrysalis and small headless meal-worms.

Strengthfood serves as supplementary food for seed-eating birds, especialy during moulting and before breeding season, to get the birds into good condition. The most beneficial kinds are available from reputable birdseed manufacturers.

Special titbits consist of wild seed like Nettle, Birch, Alder, Thistle, etc. One teaspoonfull a day.

Greenstuff weeds (gathered from land which has not been treated with chemicals), lettuce, spinach, fresh groundsel, chickweed, dandelion, pieces of carrots, etc.

Fruit ripe (not rotted) apples, pears, cherries (preferably without stones), cut grapefruit and oranges (with some concentrated feed on it), bananas, wild berries, soaked raisins and sultanas, grapes, peaches, etc.

Grit is powdered shell and is essential for a bird's digestive system. There are many good types of grit available. Oyster grit used for chickens is too coarse and not suitable for caged birds.

Lime in the form of cubes (for parrots and parakeets) and cuttlefish bone are necessary for nearly all birds especially during breeding time and moult. Cuttlefish bone found on beaches is much too salty and should be soaked in water for a few days (renew the water three times daily).

Water must be readily available. The ideal construction would be in the form of a small rock with an outlet for running water. But since such an arrangement is rather expensive (added to which the supply needs to be cut off during winter) most birdkeepers make to with clay-bowls. However, this is not a very hygienic arrangement because birds tend to bathe in them. Similarly, birds will attempt to bathe in fountains, but the problem is not so great because the water is renewed and the fountains are often too small for the birds to bathe in. Open drinking places should be covered with gauze, particularly during periods of frost. It is quite possible for birds to freeze to death during winter bathing. Therefore, regular daily checks are essential to make sure everything is alright. Bathing water must be replenished daily because the bowls quickly get dirty and need regular cleaning.

Insects including meal-worms (without heads), enchytraes, spiders, water fleas and dew-worms (gathered from ground that is free of chemicals) are all popular. They may be collected by passing a fine-meshed net against weeds and putting the resultant catch in a box. Shake the box vigorously so that the insects become stunned and can be eaten by the birds before they have a chance to escape from the aviary. Do not give bees to your birds.

Breeding of feeding material
Meal-worms should be available throughout the year, particularly during the breeding season. To breed them, you will first need to collect a few beetles. In a box of about 50×25×25cm (20×10×10in), drill three holes of approximately 3cm (1¼in) diameter on each side. Cover the inside of these holes with gauze to avoid the beetles getting out. The holes should be drilled at a height of 2cm (¾in) away from the bottom. To avoid the box rotting, line it with plastic or sheet-zinc, making sure that the

holes are left free. Cover the box with a well fitting lid, again to avoid the beetles being able to escape and also to lessen the smell. For better ventilation, drill a few holes in the lid as well. These can be a bit bigger than 3cm (1¼in). Cover the inside of the holes with gauze and the rest of the lid with plastic or sheet-zinc. When the box is ready, fill it with hacked straw up to 5cm (2in) high. On top of the straw put a piece of old towel and cover this with bran 4cm (1½in) thick. On top of the bran put another piece of old towel and again a layer of bran. Continue to about 3cm (1¼in) away from the edge of the box. Cover it all with a cloth (which must not be too thick so that the lid closes well) and finally a sheet of cardboard. On this piece of cardboard put soaked white bread, pieces of fruit or greenstuff. Once a week you can gather the meal-worms 'ready for eating' from the cardboard. Well-washed you can offer them to your birds. Don't forget that some birds must not have too many because they might get too fat and, as breeding birds, be of little or no value. You should cut off the head of worms fed to young or small birds in your aviary. This is because meal-worms swallowed alive can gnaw through a bird's crop with many unpleasant results.

Enchytraes You can find 'breeding pairs' of these creatures beneath rotting wood and leaves. They are small thin white worms. You can easily breed them in a box of 35×35×25cm (13×13×10in). Fill the box with peat and good leafy earth. The whole thing must not be too firm, but loose and not too dry. With a spade make a hole in the middle of the box of about 15cm (6in) diameter. On the bottom put a slice of soaked white bread and worms. Then cover the box with a glass lid and newspaper so that it remains dark inside. Check regularly that the bottom is not too dry and enough food is available for the Enchytraes. After a few weeks you can harvest the worms. Rinse them and you have excellent food for your birds, especially during breeding time. Temperatures for successful breeding are at around 12°C (54°F).

Maggots Only few bird-fanciers are tempted to breed maggots. I must confess it is not a pleasant business. If you have a big garden, you can use a hidden spot to hang up a piece of meat. The flies will lay eggs on it. After a few days put the meat in a tin which closes well. After another few days you will have as many maggots as you need. Don't give these immediately to the birds. Rinse them first for at least 15 minutes under a weak spray of water. This takes care of the evacuation of the maggots' intestines. The maggots then become white and can be given to the birds. Less troublesome and less unappetising is breeding maggots in preserve glasses. Fill a jar with boiled potatoes and sour milk and put it outside without a lid. After a few days close the jar. After a few more days the maggots will start developing.

Record keeping
Using an exercise book, write down anything that seems important or has significance. Keep a page for each bird in the book. With time these records become invaluable to every bird-fancier who wants to succeed in birdkeeping. If you write down everything regularly – and regularity is of the greatest importance – you will have a record of whether each pair is genetically pure or not, whether they breed well, what their feeding pattens are, whether they are quarrelsome or not, etc. It probably takes a few breeding seasons before you know sufficient about your birds. The entries might read as follows:

Cage breeding cage 27

Ring number male 72-1974

Ring number female 38-1974

Colour breeding male grey
Colour breeding female grey

Colour ring male and female blue

Notes To distinguish offspring of this pair, both senior Zebra Finches wear the colour ring on their right leg

Date of birth offspring 17.5.1975

Ring number offspring 14-1975, 15-1975, 17-1975, 18-1975 (number 16-1975 accident one week after leaving nest)

Colour ring offspring blue (left)

Colour offspring
14 grey ♂
15 grey ♂
16 grey ♂ dead
17 brown ♀
18 grey ♀

Special notes
1 externally normal grey zebras
2 male parent hands down brown, number 17 is brown female
3 parent female is a good breeding bird

Ringing

Bird-rings can be obtained from various bird associations. These are not to be confused with aluminium rings used for the scientific ringing of wild birds by members of ornithological stations and for which a special licence is required.

2 mm (.07in) Amandava subflava, Estrilda troglodytes, Orange-cheeked Waxbill, St Helena Waxbill, Red Avadavat, similar species as well as hybrids of these kinds.

2.3 mm (.08in) Astrilds, Lavender Finch, both kinds of Cuban finches, Green Singing Finch, Grey Singing Finch, Zebra Finch, all magpies, both kinds of *Lonchura striata, Euodice malabarica cantans* and Steel Finch, *Poephila cincta, Carduelis cucullata*, and all hybrids.

2.5 mm (.01in) Cut Throat Finch, all *Lonchura domestica*, Diamond Sparrow, and all hybrids.

2.9 mm (.1in) Song and Colour Canaries, Wildsong and bastards with canaries, also wildsong×wildsong, wildsong×tropical birds, the two crown finches (Red and Grey), Saffron Finch, Tanagers, Indigo Bunting, Alario Finch, Rainbow Bunting, Lazuli Bunting.

3.5mm (.13in) All nightingales, Thrushes, Bulbuls, Rice Birds, furthermore Norwich Canary, Yorkshire Canary, Lancashire Canary.

4mm (.15in) Budgerigars, Cardinals, small tropical doves, small quails, Grey-headed Mynah, Glossy Starling, Pagodah Mynah, Bourke's Parakeet, Pennant's Parakeet, Splendid Parakeet, Turquoise Parakeet, Dwarf Parrots.

4.5mm (.17in) All Love Birds.

6mm (.23in) All rosellas not mentioned earlier, big Alexander Parakeet, Monk Parakeet, Princess of Wales Parakeet, Golden-fronted Fruitsucker, Ringneck Parakeet, Brown-ear Parakeet, Bleeding-heart Pigeons, Californian and Virginia Quail.

7mm (.27in) Australian Helmet Pigeon and Bronze-winged Pigeon

8mm (.31in) Chukar Chicken.

10mm (.39in) Bride and Mandarin Duck, Golden Pheasant.

12mm (.46in) Forest Pheasant, Lady Amherst Pheasant, Nepal Pheasant, Swinhoe Pheasant, Silver Pheasant.

14mm (.54in) All big Pheasant.

Index

insectfood, 132–3
insecticides, 82
Irena puella (Fairy Bluebird), 97
Isabel Canary, *83*

Japan, birds in 29, 33, 35, 128
Java, birds from, 17, 53, 96, 119, 123
Java Beo, *119*
Java Magpie, *17*
Java Sparrow, *96*
Jendya Parakeet, 88

Kiwi, 23
Korea, 128

Lancashire Canary, 101, 134
Lagonosticta senegala (Fire Finch), *11*, *20*
Lavender Finch, *14–15*, 134
Lazuli Bunting, *82*, 134
Leafbirds see Fruitsuckers; Orange-bellied
Leiothrix lutea (Pekin Robin), 6, 7, *126*
light, 46–7, 65
lime, 133
Lizard Canary, 101–2
Lonchura malabarica acuticauda
    (Sharp-tailed Munia), 70
Lonchura punctulata (Nutmeg Finch), *80*, 89, 100
Lonchura striata domestica (Munia), *54*;
    breeding, *36*, 56–7, *69*, 70, 98, 100, *106*;
    domestication, 35; ringing, 134; for sale, 45
Long-tailed Finch, 97
Loriculus galgulus (Blue Crown Lory), *61*
Lorikeet, *66*, *67*, 79
Lory, *28*, *61*, 89, 92
Louisiana Tanager, *13*
Love Bird: breeding, 98; care of, 88–9;
    food for, 132; nests, 82; ringing, 134; see
    also Black-cheeked; Fischer's; Masked;
    Peach-faced; Red-faced
lungs, 23
Lutino Budgerigar, *69*
Lybius leucomelas, *16*

Macaw: care of, 111, 113; see also Ara;
    Military; Red and Blue
McLey, J., 85
Magpie, Java, *17*
Mandingoa nitidula (Green Twin-spot), *17*, 38
Masked Love Bird, 79
Maycao, *116*
medicine, 129
Melba Finch, *90–1*, *121*
Melopsittacus undulatus (Wild Budgerigar)
    31–2, 74
Metise, 97–8
Mexican birds, 20, *82*, 89, 100
migration, 40
Military Macaw, *112*, 113
minerals, 129, 132–3
Mitchell's Lorikeet, *66*, *67*
mites, 129, 131
Moluccan Islands, 20, 97
Monk Parakeet, 82–3, 134
moulting, 109, 129; see also feathers;
    plucking
Mouse-birds, 26
Multicoloured Finch, *40*
Multicoloured Parakeet, *113*
Munia see Lonchura; Sharp-tailed
Munich Canary, 101
mutation, 12, 54, 69
Mynah: cage for, 117; care of, 113–14, 117,
    119; food for, 114, 117; see also Common;
    Grey-headed; Hill; Pagoda; Pied

Negro Finch, *86*, *87*
Neophema e. elegans (Elegant Grass
    Parakeet), 76
Neophema pulchella (Turquoise Parakeet),
    47
Neophema splendida (Splendid Parakeet), *62*
nests, *10*, 79, 82, *105*, 106–7, 123
nest boxes, 63, 65, *74*, 76, 82–3, 86, *105*
New Caledonia, 106
New Guinea, 70, 98
New Zealand, 23
Nightingales, *52*, 134
Nigrita canipailla (Negro Finch), *87*, 88
Nonpareil see Parrot-finch
Nonpareil Bunting, *38*

North America, birds from, 13, 26, 28, 30,
    52, 56, 82, 89
Norwich Canary, 101, 134
Nutmeg Finch, *80*, 89, 100
nutrition and diseases, 123, 129; see also
    food
Nymphicus hollandicus (Cockatiel), 48, 49,
    78

Onagodori, 29
Orange-bellied Leafbird, 126, *127*
Orange-cheeked Waxbill, *54*, 56, *124*, 134
ornithosis, 126

Padda oryzivora (Java Sparrow), *96*
Pagodah Mynah, *18*, 19, 134
painting cages, 59, 61
Papaver somniferum, 129
Paradise, Birds of, 26
Parakeet: in aviary, 63, 65; baldness, 48;
    breeding, *74*, 83, 85; care of, 82–3, 85,
    88–9; domestication, 40; ringing, 94; see
    also Alexander; Bourke's; Brown-ear;
    Dwarf; Elegant Grass; Goldchin;
    Goldhead; Jendya; Monk;
    Multicoloured; Pennant's;
    Plum-headed; Princess of Wales;
    Ringneck; Rosella; Rose-ringed; Song –;
    Splendid; Tovi; Turquoise
parasites, 129, 131
paratyphus, 125
Parrot: baldness, 48; cage, 46; care of, 109,
    111; disease of, 126; food, 111, 132; see also
    African Grey; Amazon; Black-headed;
    Green Dwarf; Superb
Parrot-finch, 38, *39*, 88, 106, *108*
Parson Finch, 134
Parvaria coronata (Grey Cardinal), *67*
Passerina amoena (Lazuli Bunting), *82*
Passerina ciris (Nonpareil Bunting), *38*
Passerina cyanea (Indigo Bunting), *52*
Passerina lechancherii (Rainbow Bunting),
    22
Passerina versicolor (Multicoloured Finch),
    40
Pectoral Sparrow, *93*
Pekin Robin, 6, 7, 55, *126*, 133
Peach-faced Love Bird, *72–3*, 74
Pennant's Parakeet, 134
Peophila cincta, *87*
perches, 61, 63
pests, 37, 70
pheasants, 26, 65, 134
Pied Mynah, *53*
pigeon, 30, 32–3, 37, 40; see also
    Australian; Bleeding-heart;
    Bronze-winged; Victoria Crowned
Pionites melanocephala (Black-headed
    Parrot), *19*
Piranga ludoviciana (Louisiana Tanager),
    13
Pirenestes ostrinus (Crimson Waxbill), *93*
Pitta guajana (Banded Pitta), *130*, 131
Pitta moluccensis (Blue-winged Pitta), *7*
Pitta sordida (Hooded Pitta), *128*
plastic, 60
Platycerus e. eximius (Rosella Parakeet), *78*
Platycerus genus, 62, 100
plucking see feathers
Plum-headed Parakeet, 83
plumage see feathers
Poephila acuticauda (Long-tailed Finch),
    97
Poephila bichenovii (Doublebar Finch), *38*
Poephila cincta (Parson Finch), 134
Pogoniulus chrysoconus (Yellow-fronted
    Tinker Bird), *17*
pond, 65
Princess of Wales Parakeet, 134
protected birds see conservation
Psephotus varius (Multicoloured Parakeet),
    113
psittacosis, 126
Psittacula eupatria nipalensis (Alexander
    Parakeet), *63*
Psittacus erithacus (African Grey Parrot),
    111
Pterodactyl, *8*
Pyrrhula pyrrhula (Bullfinch), *81*
Pyrrhuloxia sinuata (Cardinal Grosbeak), *89*
Pytilia melba (Melba Finch), *90–1*, *121*

quails, 65, 134

quarantine, 45
Quelea quelea quelea (Red-billed Weaver),
    70, *71*

Rainbow Bunting, *22*, 134
Ramphastos sulfuratus (Toucan), *20*
Ramphocelus bresilius (Scarlet Tanager), *48*
records, 133–4
Red Avadavat, *123*, 134
Red Canary, *42*, 43, 97, 102, *118*
Red Crown Finch, 134
Red Jungle Fowl, 29
Red Macaw, *76*, 77
Red-billed Quelea, 70, *71*
Red-blue Ara, *116*
Red-faced Love Bird, *75*
Red-headed Starling, *22*
Red-tail Canary, 100
Red-tailed Black Cockatoo, *117*
Red-throated Twin-spot, *17*
Red-whiskered Bulbul, *96*
Red-wing Ara, *116*
Reed Finch, 100
reproduction, 11–12; see also breeding
reptiles, 13, 23
respiratory ailments, 126, 129
Rice Finch, *96*, 134
Richmondena cardinalis (Virginian
    Cardinal), *52*
ringing, 80, 92, 94, 134
Ringneck Parakeet, 134
Robin, Pekin, 6, 7, 55, *126*, 133
rodents, 125
Rogerson, Mrs., 85
Roller Canary, 53, 55
Roller, 'Harzer', 60
Rose-ringed Parakeet, 33, 83, 88
Rosella Parakeet, *78*

Saffron Finch, *37*, 134
St Helena Waxbill, *11*, 134
saurian, *8*
Scarlet Crest Siskin, 97
Scarlet Tanager, *48*
Scots Fancy Canary, 101
Seed-eater, Yellow-rumped, *50*
Serinus atrogularis (Black-throated Canary),
    50
Serinus canaria (Wild Canary), *28*, *101*
Serinus canicollis (Cape Canary), 100, *107*
Serinus leucopygius (Grey Singing Finch),
    106
Serinus mozambicus (Green Singing Finch),
    98, *99*
Setaria italica, 129
sex-linked breeding, 74
Shama, 56
Shama Thrush, *20*
Sharp-tailed Munia, 70
shops, bird, 43–6
shows, bird, *33*, *38*, *40*, *43*
Sicalis flaveola (Saffron Finch), *37*
Silverbill, African, 56–7, 100
sight, 23–4
Siskin, *80*, 97, 100
Sitagra vitellina (Yolk-yellow Weaver), *26*
skeleton, 23
songbirds, 6, 7, 17, 24–5, 33, 50, 53, 81,
    85, 96
Song-parakeets, 53, 85
South American: Ara, 114, 116; Avadavat,
    128; Humming Bird, 26; Macaw, 76,
    113; Parakeet, 33, 88, 111; Parrot, 19,
    29–30, 33–4; Siskin, 97; Starling, 22;
    Tanager, 12–13, 26, 49, 114, 116
Spain, 28, 33
Sparrow, *28*; see also Diamond; Java
    Pectoral
specialisms, 23
species numbers, 12
Spermestes genus (Magpie), *17*
Spice Bird, *80*
Splendid Parakeet, *62*, 97, 134
Sri Lanka, 19
Starling see Glossy; Red-headed; tropical
Steel Finch, 134
Steganopleura guttata (Diamond Sparrow),
    83
Sternus pagodarum (Pagodah Mynah), *18*,
    19
Strawberry Finch, *123*
Straw-yellow Canary, *104*
Sturnus contra (Pied Mynah), *53*

Sugarbird, Yellow-winged, 94
Sulphur-crested Cockatoo, *64*, *65*, 113, *116*
Sumatra, 123
Superb Parrot, *46*
Superb Tanager, *13*, *120*, 121
Surinam, 93
Swainson's Lorikeets, 79

Taeniopygia guttata (Zebra Finch), *54–5*,
    69, *122*
tail feathers, 38
talking, 74, 76, 109, 111, 113–14, 119
tameness: Budgerigar, 74–6; Canary, 101;
    Lory, 89; Macaw, 111; Mynah, 113–14,
    119; Parrot, 109; when purchasing, 45
Tangara arthus goodsoni (Golden Tanager),
    130, 131
Tangara fastuosa (Superb Tanager), *13*,
    120, 121
Tanager, 26, 56, 134; see also Blue; Fruit;
    Golden; Louisiana; Scarlet; Superb
Tasmania, 79
teeth, egg, 10
Terpisphone viridis (African Paradise
    Flycatcher), *10*
Thailand, 20
Thraupidae family, 94, 95, 123
Thraupis epsicopus (Blue Tanager), *12*
Thrush, *20*, 134
Tiaris canora (Cuban Finch), *119*, 134
Tiger Finch, *126*
Tinker Bird, *17*
Toucan, *20*
Tovi Parakeet, 88
toys, 60, 74–5
training, 74, 76, 114; see also tameness
Trichoglossus haematod mitchelii (Mitchell's
    Lorikeet), *66*, *67*
Trichoglossus haemotodus moluccanus
    (Swainson's Lorikeet), 79
tropical starlings, 55–6
tuberculosis, 123
Turdus citrina (Shama Thrush), *20*
turkey, 40
Turquoise Parakeet, *47*, 53, 97, 134
Twin-spots, *17*, *38*

United States, birds from, 13, 28, 30, 52,
    56, 82, 89
Uraeginthus bengalus (Cordon Bleu), *67*, *68*,
    69

vegetation in aviary, 63, 65, 92, 109, 132–3
Victorian Crowned Pigeon, 98
Virginian Cardinal, *52*, 56
Virginian Nightingale, *52*
virus diseases, 126
vitamins, 123, 129, 132–3

wading birds, 21
water, 57, 65, 68–9, 100, 111, 133
Waxbill, 93; see also African; Crimson;
    Orange-bellied; St Helena
Weaver, *26*, 70
West Indies, 16
White Canary, *51*, 100
White-eye, Indian, *26*, *27*
Wild Budgerigar, *31*
Wild Canary, *28*, *101*
wings, 23
woodland birds, 80, 94, 96, 132
worms, 131

Yellow Canary, 55
Yellow Roller Canary, 55
Yellow-fronted Tinker Bird, *17*
Yellow-legged Honeycreeper, *128*
Yellow-naped Yuhina, *24–5*
Yellow-rumped Seed-eater, *50*
Yellow-wing Ara, *116*
Yellow-winged Sugarbird, 94
Yolk-yellow Weaver, *26*
Yorkshire Bullfinch, 100
Yorkshire Canary, *85*, 101, 134
Yuhina flavicollis (Yellow-naped Yuhina),
    24–5

Zebra Finch, 35, *45*, *54–5*, 56, *69*, 82, 100,
    122, 134
Zoothera citrina (Shama Thrush), *20*
Zosterops palpebrosa (Indian White-eye),
    26, *27*